To Uncle Billy,

D0115697

☆ THE UNCLE BOOK ☆

JESSE COGAN is a writer, documentary filmmaker, and advertising veteran who specializes in producing advertising and promotional materials for nonprofit organizations. The winner of several major awards, including three Clios, an Effie, and a One Show Merit, Cogan has also written for *TV Guide* and *Cosmopolitan*. He, his wife, and twins live in Manhattan. His nieces and nephews live in Scarsdale, New York, and Jerusalem, Israel.

Marlowe & Company

♡ your niece ♡

☆ **JESSE COGAN** ☆

THE UNCLE BOOK

EVERYTHING YOU NEED TO KNOW TO BE A KID'S FAVORITE RELATIVE

Marlowe & Company
New York

THE UNCLE BOOK:
Everything You Need To Know To Be a Kid's Favorite Relative
Copyright © 2002 by Jesse Cogan

Published by
Marlowe & Company
An Imprint of Avalon Publishing Group Incorporated
161 William Street, 16th Floor
New York, NY 10038

All rights reserved. No part of this book may be reproduced in
whole or in part without written permission from the publisher,
except by reviewers who may quote brief excerpts in connection
with a review in a newspaper, magazine, or electronic
publication; nor may any part of this book be reproduced, stored
in a retrieval system, or transmitted in any form or by any
means electronic, mechanical, photocopying, recording, or other,
without written permission from the publisher.

Library of Congress Cataloging-in-Publication Data
Cogan, Jesse
The uncle book: everything you need to know to be a kid's
favorite relative/ by Jessy Cogan.
p. cm.
ISBN 1-56924-587-8
1. Uncle. I. Title.

HQ1090 .C64 2001
306.87—dc21   2001030022

9 8 7 6 5 4 3 2 1

Designed by Pauline Neuwirth, Neuwirth and Associates, Inc.

Printed in the United States of America
Distributed by Publishers Group West

To Naomi, Max, and Riva

CONTENTS

PREFACE

I WAS TWENTY-ONE and had just received my driver's license. My oldest nephew, Avi, was three-and-a-half years old. I had already changed and fed this kid, baby-sat him, read him stories, and bought him his first watergun. He was as comfortable with me as with anyone.

What I wanted to do now, more than anything, was take him for a ride alone in my parents' car and buy him a slice of pizza. It took some convincing, but my sister finally acquiesced.

After a series of long hugs and good-byes—the kind of farewell usually reserved for your loved ones as they board a steamship leaving for the Orient—I packed a stroller in the trunk, secured Avi in the backseat, and took off. This was years before the days of regulated car seats.

Everything I had learned in driver's ed came alive during that trip. I defensively peeked around corners, anticipated the moves of the cars around me, gave surprised pedestrians the right-of-way, and kept a careful eye on my mirrors as well as my speedometer.

Finally, we turned onto Central Avenue, a busy four-lane street with two-way traffic and a great pizzeria.

"We're here," was all I could say, relieved as we pulled alongside a parking meter across the street from our destination. I got out of the car to get the stroller out of the trunk.

Seconds later, I heard cars screeching to a halt and horns blasting. I looked up to see the most horrible sight in my history as an uncle. My tiny, precious nephew was fighting off traffic in the middle of the street as cars swerved around him and vented their outrage. While I was getting his stroller, he had opened the car door on the traffic side and headed straight for the pizza shop he knew and loved.

"Oh, God!" I thought to myself. "What the hell kind of uncle am I?"

UNCLE—*noun*—a relative
> USAGE: My mother's brother is my uncle.

UNCLE—*verb*—to act as an uncle
> USAGE: I love to uncle.

UNCLING—*verb*—the act of being an uncle
> USAGE: Uncling requires many skills.

UNCLE—*proper noun*—prefix attached to a first name
> USAGE: Uncle Billy is my uncle.

UNCLEHOOD—*noun*—a societal institution
> USAGE: Unclehood makes families stronger.

Have We Overlooked
Our Favorite Relative?

THERE ARE BOOKS about how to be a better lover, boyfriend, or handyman; how to teach, cook or drive better. You can easily find information on being a better father, grandfather, or even sibling. Yet when it comes to being an uncle, there are no handbooks or analyses; no encyclopedia, articles, or Cliff notes.

Despite the fact that there are more uncles in America than fathers, more nephews and nieces than sons and daughters, and the largest population of unmarried men ever in our society, no one seems to care about this lack of guidance. Uncling gets less attention than lesbians, lepers, lawyers, or landladies. Punch it up on an Internet search and you'll get few, if any, results. Books, magazines, or journal abstracts—nothing.

You might find some information here and there about African-American families that put uncles in charge of moral guidance due to a fatherless family unit. Or how it is Hindu practice to put the mother's brother in charge of screening prospective brides and grooms for their nephews and nieces. If you dug deep enough, you'd probably come across something on Shia Islam marriage, where uncles and nieces are encouraged to marry one another, or other lesser-known societies where uncles play specific, sometimes unusual, ascribed roles in family life.

But generally, in Western society, every uncle shapes his own relationship, using his own creativity, building his own model. The role is one of achievement, not ascription. You play it the way you want. You are defined neither by behavior nor by predetermined criteria. You decide how often you should visit and whether you should bring gifts, send cards, or acknowledge birthdays. Should you meddle, coach, encourage, or discipline? Are you clown, teacher, or friend? Do you cherish, love, and adore, or do you have to care at all?

There are no Rules of Uncle Procedure, nor do the *Bible,* the Constitution, or family court frown upon any particular uncle behavior. You won't be graded as a good uncle or a bad uncle no matter what choices you make. There's no certificate, training program, or nights in the pokey. The kind of uncle you become is entirely in your hands. You can embrace it with a full heart or you can disown it, if only you can determine what it is.

What Do We Say About Uncles?

CAN YOU NAME an uncle who's a perfect ten? What about a six? What about a father's brother who's not an uncle at all?

I'm not proposing we create a checklist of qualities that allow uncles entry into a club. We don't do that for established institutions like motherhood, fatherhood, prison, or the judicial system. Yet there are sets of expectations, unique for each role, for moms and dads, judges and prosecutors. Society does have certain expectations. It expects that Mom will take care of the kids, Dad will support the family, prisoners will have their freedom taken away, and prosecutors will get criminals off the street.

Is a prosecutor who hasn't won a case in fifteen years still a prosecutor? Perhaps, but not a very good one.

Do a deadbeat dad who refuses to pay child support or a mom who refuses to kiss a boo-boo live up to their roles? Hardly.

How much money does an uncle need to spend annually to maintain his status? How often should he visit, and how long should he stay? Must he know how to play cards? Wiggle his ears? Tell bedtime stories into the night?

Can a gambler be an uncle? What about a common thief? Must an uncle believe in God, or can he be agnostic? Should an uncle be an athlete, an avid reader, a crossword puzzle solver, or a homemaker? Can he be rich and famous? Can he be short? Can he be gay?

Should you exchange gifts at Christmas? Must you be invited to your nephew's Bar Mitzvah? There is no established code of behavior; no norms, no rules nor ordinances, no real expectations about being an uncle at all.

What exactly do uncles accomplish? What's in it for them, for the kids, for the family, for society?

THE MEANING OF UNCLE

TAKE A MOMENT to reflect on what the word uncle means in these contexts:

→ A major news magazine headlined an article about how corporations help female employees by providing day-care centers at work. The title of the article read, "Kinder Care Turns Employers into Uncles."

→ A carpet retailer spent hundreds of thousands of TV advertising dollars to attract buyers to a sale. The hook: "You have an uncle in the carpet business."

→ Thomas Burke, the popular essayist, wrote a tribute to Saturday, the seventh day of the week. His title: "An Uncle of a Day."

☆

Uncle: The Elusive Prefix

PUT IT IN front of a name, and it takes on a whole new meaning. Uncle Miltie. Uncle Scrooge. Uncle Sam.

Is there a common thread?

Uncle Scrooge is hardly known for his benevolence. Uncle Miltie was far more bizarre than charming. And when Uncle Sam comes collecting for the IRS or pointing at you to sign up for the army, your feelings are, at best, patriotic. More likely, you want to run away.

You might be loved, despised, revered, or a huggable bear. You could be the business partner who is the source of daily complaints at the family dinner table, the ogre who refuses to make more than once-a-month nursing home visits to Grandma, or the expected guest who never arrives without the perfect gift.

Your cigar could stink up a house, your dandruff might cover the family couch, and you might be the last person in America to have discovered underarm deodorant.

It hardly matters whether you are placed high on a pedestal or never spend more than ten minutes alone with the kids; uncles play a role in family life. It is the exact nature of your role that remains somewhat elusive.

Ask any man whether he thinks he's a good uncle and you'll get mostly black-and-white answers: "I'm a great uncle" or "I'm a terrible uncle." "I have no relationship with my nephews and my nieces," or "I have a great relationship with my nephews and nieces." Few grays, few definitions of good and bad, few clearly delineated expectations. The common thread: "It's difficult to describe."

You Are Among the
First Adults Kids Get To See

CHILDREN'S EARLY EXPOSURE to flaws in adults is limited, centered around Mom and Dad. They are the people that walk around the house in their underwear and fight over who's next for the bathroom. Every other adult in their lives is on guard. Teachers couldn't possibly behave in the classroom as they do at home. The neighbors next door are as pleasant as can be when Mom pops over for a chat, but what happens after they close the door?

A child needs someone familiar to lend a different perspective.

Uncles belch generously at the table. They ignore a mom's demands to stop the teasing. They sleep over and invade the family's space. They walk into the house without ringing the doorbell, throw their ratty sports jacket onto the new family couch, and talk to respected adults like no one has before.

With familiarity comes responsibility. As an uncle, you will undoubtedly have an opportunity to help mold a child's life. You can shape a career, help develop character, coach a basketball team, change a habit, preserve a dream, or encourage a reality. A good uncle takes his responsibility seriously, even while he's having a great time.

☆

WHO WOULD YOU RATHER HAVE BABY-SIT? AN AUNT OR AN UNCLE?

IT'S TEMPTING TO look to aunts as a basis to define the role of an uncle, but uncles are definitely not the male version of an aunt. An uncle's role is too unique.

Unlike actor/actress, waiter/waitress, and even grandfather/grandmother, uncle is gender-specific. Like mother/father, sister/brothers, husband/wife, and yes, nephew/niece, your role also embodies your gender.

- ❖ Aunts nurture; they try to be moms. Uncles bond; they don't need to imitate Dad.
- ❖ Aunts are sensible; they bring fruit to the movies. Uncles buy popcorn, candy, and soda.
- ❖ Aunts count down to bedtime; uncles never watch the clock.
- ❖ Aunts put kids on their lap and read them a book. Uncles spin yarns, making up the story as they go along.
- ❖ Aunts take you to museums. Uncles take you to the circus.
- ❖ Aunts send birthday cards; uncles send e-mail.

There's nothing wrong with being an aunt. But as a man you can never own that role. Nor, I imagine, would you want to.

★

You Shape Lives

WHILE MOM AND Dad are busy with the difficult day-to-day routine of rearing the children, instilling values, giving their children knowledge, and trying desperately to get them to see things their way, you shake it all up with a whole new perspective. You do not have the responsibility of raising the children. Your relationship is more sporadic. You are therefore less likely to disappoint than moms and dads, less likely to frustrate.

Going to an amusement park with you is far more entertaining than going with the immediate family. Having you read them a book, tie their shoelaces, or snuggle up with them while watching a video is much different, much more enlightening, and a lot more memorable than when Mom and Dad do it.

You can play a major or minor role in a variety of key areas, such as career, social relationships, financial savvy, and personality. You offer new information, new perspectives, and new ways of reacting to the world. You encourage and motivate, model values and rituals. You link generations by being partners with your siblings, the grandparents, and the kids themselves.

If your brother-in-law is a klutz, your nephews and nieces might look to you for examples of agility. If your sister overuses discipline, the kids might look to you as offering a freer way of

The Uncle in Culture
and History

LET'S LOOK AT fictional uncles like Scrooge, Ben, Vanya, Buck, and Tom, or uncles in American history like our only bachelor president, James Buchanan, who in the glorious days of nineteenth century White House entertaining had his orphaned niece, Harriet Lane, serve brilliantly as First Lady. And Colonel George Ross, who showed up at his niece Betsy's doorstep along with General George Washington and asked her to embroider the American flag.

Famous writers, such as Joseph Conrad, Somerset Maugham, and Jonathan Swift, were raised by uncles when their own parents died. Walter Farley, whose *Black Stallion* sold millions of copies, said he "learned to understand horses" at his uncle's riding academy.

Uncles have inspired creativity in tangible ways, like the uncle of Copernicus, the fourteenth century astronomer who sent his nephew to a university to study mathematics. Because of this uncle, we now know that the Earth spins on its axis and revolves around the sun.

And President Rutherford B. Hayes got his chance to go to Harvard Law School because his uncle paid his tuition.

The *Bible* offers some classic uncles, such as Abraham, who when asked by God to leave his people and his home to find a new land, decided to take along just one person in addition to his immediate family: his nephew Lot.

And at least one uncle in antiquity inspired greatness—the uncle of the Muslim prophet Mohammed, who raised him as a child after he was orphaned.

A stubborn Chicago gangster uncle was killed by his Brooklyn nephew when he refused to go along with demands to add bootlegging to their thriving prostitution and gambling efforts. The new mobster who replaced this hapless uncle was the most famous gangster of them all: Al "Scarface" Capone.

The word uncle has also become part of our daily vocabulary. We cry uncle when we give up in a fight, probably because as kids we were tickled by our uncles until we begged them to stop. We are as astonished as a monkey's uncle; people who talk to us sternly are Dutch uncles; people who treat us nicely are rag uncles.

We sing songs like Stephen Foster's "Uncle Ned." Retail stores use it in their names: Uncle Bob's Pizza, Uncle Sam's Shoe Repair, Uncle Max's Mattress Factory.

In 1939, Hollywood's coveted Oscar award was named after Academy of Motion Pictures executive director Margaret Herrick's uncle Oscar, after she remarked that the statue resembled him.

Uncles abound in entertainment; Uncle Miltie, *My Favorite Martian*, Paul Newman's Hud, Uncle John's Band; The Beatle's Uncle Albert, Uncle Jed of *The Beverly Hillbillies*, Frankenstein-like Uncle Herman of *The Munsters*, and Uncle Charlie of *My Three Sons*.

And unlike cake mixes, owned by the females, instant rice belongs to Uncle Ben.

An American Logo:
UNCLE SAM

TALL, BEARDED, and colorful, few things represent the United States more than the image of Uncle Sam. He recruits us, urges us to pay taxes, and solicits good citizenship. But actually, he is only the figment of a cartoonist's imagination. James Montgomery Flag created him along with a nephew, Jonathan, in the early 1800s. Jonathan eventually was dropped, but Uncle Sam has been an American icon ever since.

being. If your sibling's marriage is rocky, they might look to you for stability. You are more than a friend, different from a next-door neighbor. You are a relative; you are family. And like it or not, as an uncle, you have an impact on your nephews' and nieces' lives.

You Benefit From Being An Uncle

BEING AN UNCLE allows you to interact with the younger generation without dealing with their baggage or the emotional baggage your own children carry. By acting out with your nieces and nephews, you get to show affection and love for siblings, even those with whom you haven't gotten along in years. Uncling lets you guide and encourage; it lets you take someone close under your wing without being held completely responsible. It gets your jokes laughed at and your stories appreciated. It extends your family.

Is uncling a learned or an acquired skill? How can we predict an uncle's success in his role? Why do some uncles get more respect than others? And how important is this whole relationship anyway?

The Uncle Book will explore and validate your role by putting it in perspective within the extended family and society and by giving it the credit it deserves.

You will examine how your personality affects your performance, what rules and expectations apply, and how the unique uncle bond is formed. *The Uncle Book* offers suggestions, tips, exercises, and anecdotes. It looks at the many styles of being an uncle, its rewards, its challenges, and the real difference an uncle can make in the life of a child that he loves.

You'll learn to think like an uncle, sing like an uncle, even burp a baby like an uncle. You'll learn to tell uncle stories and share uncle adventures. You will test your skills and learn how to maximize your performance. You'll learn ways to renew your bond with your siblings, develop new alliances with your family, and get in touch with a side of yourself you might never have explored.

You will become a better uncle, and somewhere along the way, a kid's favorite relative.

UNCLEDOTE

A Lesson in Underwear
—You Do Have a Choice

AT THE TENDER *age of three, I was under the mistaken impression that there was only one way for a grown man to dress beneath his pants—boxer shorts. It was what my father wore, in different pastel colors, every day.*

My Uncle Jack, however, introduced me to the world of options.

One morning, following a wonderful uncle night when my then-single uncle not only visited us for the evening, but slept over as well, I woke up early and excited. As we had agreed the night before, I snuck into the guest bedroom and slipped under his quilt to be next to him.

Two ridiculously contrived stories and a couple of tickle matches later, my uncle jumped out of bed, finally ready to face the day. And there he stood wearing briefs: Little, short, crotch-hugging pieces of cotton, with a red line running through a snappy piece of elastic at the waist. It was unlike anything I had ever seen.

"Are those your pajamas?" I asked incredulously.

"Pajamas? These are my underwear," he said. And then he laughed. He remembered that my father wore boxer shorts and slept in silk nightclothes.

After some elucidation about men's style of underwear, I decided that briefs were for me. To this day, I can't get myself to wear those sexy and supposedly appealing designer boxers.

THE UNCLE QUIZ
How Good an Uncle Are You?

1. Your nine-year-old niece just had her ears pierced and asks you for a pair of earrings for her birthday. You've never bought a pair of earrings before in your life. Should you:

    A. Buy her a game instead?

    B. Shop with your girlfriend?

    C. Venture out on your own and find the perfect pair?

    D. Take her out alone one evening and shop together for a pair you both love?

2. It's your niece's sweet sixteen, and she's only invited teenage friends. How do you celebrate?

    A. You don't. You weren't invited.

    B. Send a card.

    C. Send her a gift certificate from her favorite store.

    D. Take her out to dinner alone after the party's over.

3. You promised to take your eight-year-old nephew to a baseball game on Saturday. On Wednesday he calls to ask whether he can bring along a friend. Do you:

    A. Feel hurt? You wanted to spend time with your nephew alone.

    B. Say "no problem?" Two kids are better than one.

    C. Bring along a friend of your own?

D. Say "absolutely not?" This is more responsibility than you bargained for.

4. Your nine-year-old niece has been studying the piano for months and finally gives you a private recital. She is terrible. Should you:

    A. Stand and applaud when it's over?

    B. Put her on your lap and share anecdotes about how difficult it is to master an instrument?

    C. Tell her she needs some practice?

    D. Invite her to perform at the next family party at your home?

5. Your sister just told the kids that they can't have dessert until they do their homework. Should you:

    A. Agree with Mom on how important homework is?

    B. Whine "Aw, Mom!" along with the kids?

    C. Offer to help the kids with their homework?

    D. All of the above.

6. You are baby-sitting your seven-year-old and nine-year-old nieces. How do you spend the time?

    A. Catch up on your office work and let them occupy themselves.

    B. Put them to bed early and watch an R-rated video.

    C. Rent a kids' video and watch it with them.

    D. Bake a cake together.

7. Your nephew is missing one basketball card to complete a set. Should you:

    A. Tell him to stop wasting time on nonsense?

    B. Give him ten packs as a gift and hope the missing card will be there?

    C. Buy as many packs as it takes to find the right card. Discard all the others and gift wrap the missing card?

    D. Take him to a basketball game to see the player live?

8. It's time to send out your wedding invitations. Is your policy:

    A. One invitation for each sibling family?

    B. No kids?

    C. Each nephew and niece gets an invitation of his or her own?

    D. Adult nieces and nephews only?

9. Your eight-year-old nephew wants a bedtime story. It's way past his bedtime. Should you:

    A. Refuse and say, "It's time to go to bed?"

    B. Make one up as you go along?

    C. Read him something boring and hope it puts him to sleep?

    D. Tell him a story about his great-grandfather that he never heard?

10. Your very responsible seventeen-year-old niece is spending the weekend at your house and wants to borrow your car. Her parents said it's all right with them if it's all right with you. Do you decide:

    A. She must be home by midnight?

    B. She must tell you where she's going, who she's going with, who will be there, and when she'll get back?

    C. She should be home at a reasonable hour, but if it's very late, to call?

    D. Absolutely not? Why take a chance with your car?

Scoring

Now add up the value of each answer you chose.

Question 1	(A) 1	(B) 2	(C) 3	(D) 4
Question 2	(A) 1	(B) 3	(C) 2	(D) 4
Question 3	(A) 2	(B) 4	(C) 3	(D) 1
Question 4	(A) 3	(B) 2	(C) 1	(D) 4
Question 5	(A) 1	(B) 2	(C) 3	(D) 4
Question 6	(A) 2	(B) 1	(C) 3	(D) 4
Question 7	(A) 1	(B) 2	(C) 3	(D) 4
Question 8	(A) 3	(B) 1	(C) 4	(D) 2
Question 9	(A) 1	(B) 3	(C) 2	(D) 4
Question 10	(A) 3	(B) 2	(C) 4	(D) 1

What your score means:

35-40

You can be my uncle anytime! You'll be remembered as someone special. You go that extra mile and care about each of your nephews and nieces individually. You don't take your uncling for granted. You've bunkled!

25-30

Congratulations! You take your uncling seriously. Your nephews and nieces should appreciate you. You play your role well. Try being a little more creative in your relationship. Don't always come up with the obvious solutions; it'll be worth the effort.

15-20

C'mon! You're just getting by. Uncling is fun!
Sure, you're a responsible adult. But you're an uncle, too. Think twice before you do something. Try to think like an uncle and deal with issues in a special way. You're not a neighbor from down the street. Don't be ordinary!

BELOW 15

Are you really an uncle? There's more to being an uncle than having a sibling with kids. Do what's right for your nephews and nieces. You'll soon see that you gain as much as they do.

1

Uncling Starts a Generation Before the Baby Is Born

The Power of the Sibling Relationship

TO BE AN effective uncle, you need to gain access and develop trust. Without these, you'll never get close enough to make a difference. And since the only people who can grant you both of these elements are moms and dads, you'd better take a long, hard look at where your sibling relationships stand.

How you are portrayed to the kids when you are not around, how comfortable you are made to feel when you are around, and the frequency of invitations and desired length of visits are all out of your control. They are determined by the children's parents.

Whether you're successful or a failure, sensitive or selfish, playful or stodgy, rotten or exemplary, it's usually blamed on your parents. But like the parental bond, even if you're angry, disassociated, or out of touch, the sibling bond continues.

Siblings generally grow up under the same roof, often close in age, educated in similar institutions, exposed to the same values, sharing the same experiences—especially in their early, formative years; this certainly has an effect. Siblings are the people with whom you share fifty percent of your genes, your history and family, your parents, your hurts, and your joys. Study your sibling relationships and you will find unbelievable insights into other relationships in your life, with your spouse, employer, children, and yourself. And certainly, you will begin to uncover the dynamics of your relationship with your nephews and nieces.

Sibling relationships are also among the hardest to talk about. Why? Because the feelings involved are almost always ambivalent. It is in our sibling relationships that we first test our feelings and virtues; loyalty, competition, our need for attention, and our ability to share.

Most studies indicate that siblings are more dissimilar than similar. Not only in eye color, hair color, and posture, but in personality, values, and vision as well. Academically, one's usually an achiever and the other is a dropout. Psychologically, one is often needy, while the other is independent. Professionally, one may be a lawyer, and the other a carpenter. Socially, one is a loner, and the other is a party animal.

Parents develop an understanding of sibling personality differences early on, individualizing their children, dubbing one the quiet one and the other the loud one; one ambitious and the other one lazy, as if children can be labeled in such black-and-white terms.

Two siblings who grow up in the same house and witness the same family event might emerge with radically different perceptions of it because, ultimately, personalities are formed by a wide variety of factors, and the genetic bond is just one of many influences.

The result is that as siblings grow into adults, their friends, chosen lifestyles, dreams, and the distance they choose to live from one another may result in their growing apart. Nevertheless, the psychological effects of the sibling relationship continue to influence each person's personality and growth throughout their life.

Once siblings reach adulthood, the bond between them might weaken or strengthen, but certainly it will change. Failing to recognize sibling weaknesses is often the root of unfair expectations, misunderstanding, and general family strife.

Sibling closeness is rarely distributed equally. Stephen P. Bank and Michael D. Kahn, two sibling experts, believe that "two people will inevitably seek closeness, even fusion, leaving the third person to fend for him or herself."[1]

[1] Bank, S. P. and Kahn, M. D. *The Sibling Bond*. HarperCollins: New York, NY. 1982.

Actually, this is not regarded as a negative phenomenon for the sibling left "out in the cold." He or she often breaks away by choice, sometimes unwittingly using a family squabble for an excuse, looking for independence or growth through the distance created. The other siblings, no matter how far away they move or how different their lifestyles, generally remain devoted to one another.

Regardless of what type of relationship you had with your siblings as kids, it is the quality of your adult relationships that affects you most as an uncle. Since no two sibling relationships are alike, no two relationships with any set of nephews or nieces are alike.

That's exactly how it was in my family.

My Frustrated Uncling

AS KIDS, MY brother and I, although four years apart, were as close as you can imagine.

To illustrate, consider the unusual discoloring that appeared and reappeared on the wall along my bed in our shared bedroom.

Mom tried to remove the spot with whatever cleaning fluids were being touted at the time. They always worked initially— rendering the stain practically gone—but the discoloration would reappear a week later. She would clean the area week after week, but the mark kept coming back.

Eventually, we accepted the discolored wall as part of family life. It took years before we finally figured out the cause. Because my brother was older, our bedtimes were different, as were our allowances and our privileges. Every night, until early adolescence, Hirsh would refuse to fall asleep until I came in to go to bed. Seconds later, he would grab his blanket, jump into my bed, and cuddle with me until he fell asleep. When dawn broke, one of us would notice, and Hirsh would head back to his own bed and go back to sleep. This procedure was neither planned nor spontaneous; it was simply the way we slept at night. Its origin is as much a mystery as why you wiggle your toes.

As we grew older, the small twin mattress became more and more crowded. Hirsh had to be careful not to fall off the side, which he sometimes did. I would crunch closer and closer to the wall. But eventually, we would find a comfortable spot and call it a night.

The mark? It was the outline of my body against the wall. My mother could scrub and scrub, but it would never go away because its cause was repeated again and again, night after night.

Years later, my brother kept his kids—Jennifer Dana, Jonathan Daniel, and Jason David—named with the same initials as if they were to share towels throughout life, at arm's length from me. Oh, I am very much their uncle, proud of how pretty and handsome they are; I will do anything to get a smile or a laugh from them, but the harder I try, the less I succeed.

I know little of their likes and dislikes (certainly not firsthand), and have trouble buying appropriate gifts. We make only brief small talk on the phone, and I need travel directions when I visit. The reason: A bonded, rich, and wonderful brother relationship between their father and me became distant as we became adults.

At family gatherings I would carefully approach my nieces and nephews, rubbing their smooth, delicate baby skin against my scratchy face, feeling the continuity of my family. But I was cautious, overly so, in holding, playing, and bonding. The emotional and physical distance between me and my brother's family led me to act awkward and unspontaneous, not the way an uncle should be, and certainly not the uncle I wanted to be.

Although some families have real chasms, deep animosities, and don't speak with each other for years, that was hardly my predicament. Sunday gatherings at the family beach house, weddings, and traditional occasions, along with the occasional invitation to visit, are my welcome meeting grounds with Hirch's kids.

I am writing these words on November 8th. The last time I saw the kids was last June. I long to be closer.

My Difficult But Loving Older Sister

WHEN MY SIBLINGS and I started to grow into teenagers, my mother gave my sister Rebecca unearned responsibilities. "You are the oldest, most responsible, and most mature of the children," she probably told her. She was given authority over "the boys."

All this set the stage for some loud and open sibling rivalry. Mom shared confidences with Rebecca, and Rebecca would tease, "I know something you don't know." She would run to my mother with ridiculous accusations of how I did this or that and why I should be punished. I resented her unearned authority; my mother encouraged it. Naturally, our relationship was a volatile one.

Rebecca worked horrors on my self-esteem. One of my fingers—a lifelong souvenir resulting from a kindergarten skirmish, swollen and left with only half a nail—was more than just a flaw to her. It was "so disgusting that no woman will ever hold your hand." My breath smelled, my toes had ugly little black things between them, and "he eats snot out of his nose."

"Oh no, oh no," she would cry, prancing around the house hysterically. "He touched me. He touched me."

Rebecca married young, thank God, and was out of the house by the time I was seventeen. She divorced eighteen years later, soon after moving her family to Jerusalem. To this day, it's dangerous to leave us alone in a room together for more than twenty minutes.

Two decades earlier, my sister had given birth to her first child. What joy! I was about twenty years old at the time, no feelings yet of having been single too long, no regrets yet of not having a family of my own. The only possible obstacle in getting close to Avi, Dani, and Yonina was that with each visit, I would have to live through bickering with my sister, now more hysterical than ever. The constant blowups between us were as predictable as ever; volatile, distressing, and often unmanageable.

We argued about what she should make for dinner, how sloppily I kept her spare bedroom, how much a woman should know about operating a VCR, and where she put her glasses. The important stuff.

We both had to be right and hated to be wrong. She would whine, stomp her feet, and charge out of the room. I would raise my voice, roll my eyes, or ignore her.

Nonetheless, I felt at home in her house. We never argued about her kids. She allowed me to give and receive unconditional love. Her love for me, too, so difficult to see when viewed from the surface, came through loud and clear in my relationship with my nephews and nieces. I eagerly took them places, together and individually, fed them, teased them, tickled them, and helped with their homework. I learned to support them through unique trials and tribulations, to guide them, and easily slipped into an adult relationship with each as they grew older. I cherished my relationship with each of them.

But the bickering and fights with my sister continue. My finger is as repulsive now as it ever was. I'm still never neat enough to eat at her table, and she still screams, "I'm not your maid," when I leave a mess behind.

Rebecca and I thrived on confrontation. Although the results were boisterous and hostile, belligerent and contentious, the feelings were honest. In retrospect, they were probably the most honest and open feelings I had in my work and personal relationships. No approvals, no competitions, no watching your words. Just a lot of love and a lot of slamming doors, and the bond continues to grow.

Yes, I still wish she'd shut her mouth and lose some of her nuttiness, but Rebecca has shared her children with me passionately. Often, tears will well up in her eyes when we talk about the kids. Like searching for oil in a shale field, it took some substantial digging to find the depth of our commitment, but it is there.

When my sister divorced, I was angry. But I wouldn't allow my feelings to get in the way of my uncling. Jonesy, as we called Yonina, was still young. But I met with Avi and Dani individually, one at an outdoor cafe and one in the sauna of the Jerusalem Hilton Hotel. They never quite opened up, too confused by conflicting loyalties, unexpressed anger, guilt, and betrayal; but they felt safe with me. The uncle bond was tighter than ever, not a bit unraveled by the storm raging within them.

Adult siblings often unknowingly use their sibling's kids to express feelings they should have let go of long ago. Can one deny that the role of family dynamics, the held grudges, the refusals to forgive, the deep hurts, and the unspoken resentments that are common obstacles in the uncling role? Or the fact that deep love and commitment, full acceptance, and open communication of feelings are the hallmarks of quality bonding?

Hurt feelings affect an uncle's ability to uncle. It takes a special, loving uncle to separate his role as brother and put on his uncle hat when necessary.

Fix your sibling relationships if you can. It's worth the effort. And believe in the extended family. It's what makes uncling the joy that it is.

UNCLEDOTE

Turned Tables

RUTHIE HAD A *competitive relationship with Jimmy from the time they were kids. Uncle Jimmy had always been tagged "the ambitious one," while Ruthie was "the lazy one." There was no open hostility between them, but unquestionably, Ruthie developed an attitude. Anything Jimmy did, she wanted to do better. And she succeeded.*

Today, Ruthie has a more expensive house, a nicer car in her garage, and two beautiful boys. Uncle Jimmy is childless. Luckily, Jimmy doesn't look to his sister for his self-esteem. But what does disturb him is how Ruthie's competitive nonsense creeps into his cherished relationship with his nephews.

Here's an example:

Uncle Jimmy had been longing to see the boys and made a scheduled visit. Mike and Timmy were ready to charge out into the backyard to toss around the football he had brought them, when Jimmy noticed Timmy's long, blue sneaker laces flapping around his ankles untied. He mildly lectured his nephew on the dangers of running around with untied shoelaces.

Ruthie exploded. "Don't you tell him what to do, Jimmy. He's my son, you know."

FULL SPEED AHEAD

THE BUNKLE:
THE SPECIAL UNCLE BOND

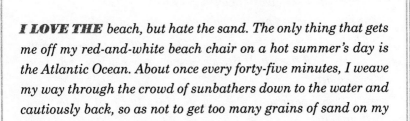

I LOVE THE beach, but hate the sand. The only thing that gets me off my red-and-white beach chair on a hot summer's day is the Atlantic Ocean. About once every forty-five minutes, I weave my way through the crowd of sunbathers down to the water and cautiously back, so as not to get too many grains of sand on my legs.

One Sunday, my brother and his kids joined me and my parents on the beach as a ninety-three degree sun beat down brutally. My bonding opportunities with my brother's kids were difficult to come by, but I knew that someday, somehow, I would be offered an opportunity. I had no idea, however, that it would happen in the middle of an impossible heat wave.

"Uncle Jesse, would you help me dig for sand crabs?"

I melt when I'm called Uncle. Eight-year-old Jennifer, with her pail, two shovels, and a long brown ponytail, looked at me longingly. I was probably her last resort. Nobody else dared move off their chairs.

First, I hesitated. I knew exactly what digging for sand crabs meant. Up to your elbows in mushy, shelly stuff, down on your hands and knees, as the ocean's waves splash in and out, spreading the mess around. And the crabs? Why would anyone want to chase after those anonymous, scurrying little blobs that bury themselves in the mud faster than you can scoop them up?

"Look, there's one, Uncle Jesse! Don't let him get away! Don't let him get away!" She squealed with delight.

That's right. I didn't pass up even this miserable opportunity to spend some precious time with my niece.

The minimonsters jumped off our shovels into the large water-filled hole we created. She called it a swimming pool. The sun beat down, and the sand discovered new parts of my body into which to settle.

We talked about why some crabs were big and some were small. Whether they had mothers and fathers. If they knew we were trying to catch them. And why they insisted on living at the beach. Later, I asked her how much admission she thought we could charge to our swimming pool.

"Twenty dollars," she said. "Twenty dollars." Then quickly changed her mind. "No, a dollar, a dollar!"

We had bunkled.

★

Are Uncles Born or Bred?

IS THE BUNKLE a biological gift or a learned skill? The result of diligence or of inclination? I wouldn't deny that there are biological components to being an uncle. The Talmud, the Jewish collection of law and wisdom, says that to determine what your children will be like, take a good look at the bride's brother. After all, nieces and nephews do share up to twenty-five percent of their uncle's genes. Physical and personal inherited traits, such as eye and hair color, mood, and mannerisms, are often shared by an uncle and his nieces and nephews. But these physical traits are hardly what constitute the bunkle.

The uncle bond is about shared feelings, circumstances, and experiences. It's about being an adult, a clown, and a friend, all at the same time. It means being there for a kid in a way unique to any other relationship they develop through their lifetime. It's about more than creating a bond; it's about creating a bunkle.

Different Uncles, Different Bunkles

I BUNKLED WITH my sister's kids at the burping and feeding stage. It's a messy way to bunkle, but it's a solid, although nonmutual, beginning. Newborns, after all, have no interest in anything beyond their mother's breast. But holding a baby, praying for a belch, or cleaning spit-up from your dark blue suit jacket can be the beginning of a bunkle; an emotional bunkle that continues to grow and mature.

A friend of mine had never bunkled with his out-of-town niece, but finally did one summer when she showed up in his New York law office looking for a summer job. Working together side by side was a bunkle.

I know a bachelor uncle who never made his bed and didn't even have a kettle in his house to boil water. He bunkled with his little nephew when he reluctantly but dutifully had him sleep over the night his sister went to the hospital to have a second baby. Sharing an anxiety was a bunkle.

And, there's the legendary long-lost uncle who bunkles at first sight with his beautiful, long-lost niece, although neither has ever laid eyes on each other before. Resolving hurt, restoring family feeling, and sharing an eager inquisitiveness about one another is a bunkle.

When you make yourself familiar to children, whether that familiarity is caused by biology, friendship, or personality, you are an uncle.

A baby girl's mother holds up her infant to a close friend and coos, loud enough for everyone to hear, "Say hello to Uncle Lester" or "Uncle Dave, would you like to hold the baby for a while?"

Now, as a nonfamily member, you surely have not yet established a relationship with this five-week-old baby. You are, after all, just a friend. And even if you were a sibling, the infant hardly internalizes this new-found uncle title. Yet by designating you "uncle," your friends or relatives invite you to share in that child's life, to be comfortable around them. You will always be a part of them. You are familiar.

A senior producer at an ad agency where I worked was especially good at mentoring young producers. We called him Uncle Walter. A camp head counselor is often called uncle. And so is the old man down the block who makes a quarter magically appear from your left ear. Your personality, too, can make you a "rag" uncle.

Walking down Broadway one Sunday, on Manhattan's busy upper west side, a voice called after me, "Uncle Jesse. Uncle Jesse." It was Elizabeth, the new bride of a very old friend. She had recently announced her pregnancy.

A bit surprised to be called uncle and frankly not connecting it at all to her pregnancy, I was taken aback. Elizabeth opened her pocketbook. She had just come from the doctor. "Want to see the baby?" she asked. She handed me a sonogram of her expected child.

I was a rag uncle because of friendship.

UNCLEDOTE

Rag Family

UNCLE LOU WASN'T *a member of our family, but nobody was more of an uncle to me. When he retired, he used his extra time to start an unofficial library club in his neighborhood. Through the sheer force of his charm and personality, he attracted teenagers, one by one, to his living room to discuss books, ideas, and the events of the day.*

About nine of us met each Wednesday night for two-and-a-half years, and Uncle Lou brought us closer to him and closer to each other. He made no judgments, and we felt like adults. You could say things in his living room that you would never say in your own home. He walked with a limp and once showed us his war wound. Lou made us feel safe.

Lou referred to himself as uncle, and we felt comfortable with it. "If you're our uncle," we laughed, "then we're all cousins." Lou had turned us into a family.

By the time we were out of college, the cousins lost touch and Uncle Lou had retired to Florida. Each of us, however, in our travels to Miami—by way of Disneyland or through phone calls and letters—had managed to stay in touch with Uncle Lou.

Our own contact with each other, sadly, didn't survive. Uncle Lou died at the age of eighty-four. The funeral was in New York, and all the cousins attended. It was the first time we had seen each other in years. Biological or not, Lou was still our uncle.

★

A Less Complicated Bond

THERE IS A fluidity to parent bonding; a complex relationship based on personality, discipline, circumstances, and environment. Isolated experiences may have some effect, but the quality of the bond will remain the same. Piece by piece, kids and their parents put their experiences into one big pie, and that pie becomes the parental bond. Family outings are as important as discipline. Carousels are as important as cleanliness. The beach is as important as the backyard. Life itself plays the key role in the parent–child bonding experience.

The bunkle is less complex, the result of a multitude of separate, mostly unrelated, and usually sporadic experiences. What good bunkling demands, unlike the parental bond, is that each nephew or niece experience be special.

Parental activity could not, and should not, be held up to that kind of scrutiny. That's one reason parents complain that uncles have it too easy. They rile up the kids before bedtime, but leave before the tantrums start. They let them skip the vegetables and feed them popcorn. They allow kids to stay up late and watch a video and forget to do their homework. Sure kids love their uncles. Who wouldn't?

I'm not suggesting that this is necessarily appropriate uncling behavior, although I don't see why not. It's certainly more acceptable than when a parent acts that way. Uncles, limited in their exposure to the kids, must maximize every moment and be open to every opportunity. You can't bunkle by pushing peas down their mouth or getting them into bed by a certain time. Bunkling is different. You bunkle through shared moments and events, conversations and behavior; moments that are uniquely yours. A shared experience, a special nickname, a secret code, or a unique way to answer the telephone can each be important elements of the bunkle.

It's Never Too Early To Form the Bunkle

HOW EARLY SHOULD the bunkle be formed? Should you show up at the hospital? Burp the baby? Diaper or feed him?

Babies will probably not do any bonding with you at this early stage, but your bond, although nonmutual, could begin. This bonding, even if not yet truly a bunkle, could be important for the future. And besides, wouldn't it be a great bunkle to share with your niece, just before she walks down the aisle at her wedding, that you used to diaper her when she was a baby.

That first smile, holding that bundle in your arms cheek to cheek, or even a frown will start your bond, if not the baby's. These experiences will increase your desire to bunkle, and you will begin to look forward to all the shared experiences that the future holds.

Early bonds accomplish another important thing: They announce and establish your intentions to the rest of the family. You are an uncle, and you are reserving your rights! You will soon start learning about your extended family. Believe me, if they don't want you at the hospital or to hold the baby too long, you will know it. Now is the time to find out.

Get as involved or be as standoffish as you like at this early stage. But as an uncle you must know, there's nothing as delicious as a sweet-smelling baby cuddled against your body.

How to Uncle to
Newborns and Infants

INFANTS SLEEP, CRY, eat, burp, and excrete. When they pass gas, they mischievously smile, and their untrained digestive and respiratory systems create a symphony of noises; snorts, grunts, sighs, and coos.

Don't let a baby's cry concern you; it's merely their way of communicating. It could mean anything from, "change my diaper," "feed me," or "burp me," to "something's sticking me in the leg."

Tips on Handling a Baby
- ☛ Support baby's head and neck—newborn and infant necks are very delicate, and they tend to wobble.
- ☛ Support baby's back—it's weak.
- ☛ Warm up your hands and be gentle—skin is sensitive.
- ☛ Let them hear your heartbeat.
- ☛ Carry around a towel or cloth diaper—they spit up.

What You Need To Burp a Baby
- ☛ A comfortable position
- ☛ A cloth to protect you from spit-up
- ☛ Patience

How To Soothe a Crying Baby
- ☛ Feed (unless Mom is nursing)
- ☛ Burp
- ☛ Change
- ☛ Stand
- ☛ Rock
- ☛ Sing
- ☛ Hand her back to Mom

Bunkle moments should be yours, as exclusive to you as possible. Few kids will forever remember the day you came to the family barbecue. Nor will they cherish your appearance at the school play or helping them blow out the candles at their third birthday party. But they will treasure how you taught them to flip a burger, when you told them to "break a leg," or the time you decorated their birthday cake with those ridiculous candles they couldn't blow out.

But finding "firsts" within shared family experiences is too much of a challenge. The bigger event—the barbecue, school production, or birthday party—is often too overpowering to find that special moment. Typically, these events are marred by competition with other people, each with their own agenda, such as grandparents, aunts, other uncles, cousins, neighbors, and friends. Better to isolate the experience. Individualize. Personalize.

Although most "firsts" are reserved for parents—like riding a bike or going to a baseball game—sometimes individual parents lack a particular skill or the patience to teach their kids some technique or game, and you can bunkle with that. It's unlikely that a parent will be unable to teach his or her child to tie a shoe, but they might not know how to throw a football.

Often, your sibling can give you the perfect opening to share one of those "firsts" with your niece or nephew: "Go ask Uncle Max to show you how to tie a bow tie." "Watch how Uncle Danny twirls pasta around his spoon." "Uncle Sammy's in real estate. Do you think you can beat him at Monopoly?" "Watch how Uncle

Dennis does pushups: He works out in a gym every day."

These words are golden. This is where an uncle can shine. But relying solely on your brothers and sisters to supply you with bunkling opportunities is like building an accountant practice on your relatives and friends. It can be profitable, even successful. But it will never grow beyond your dreams.

Some "Firsts" for Bunkling

- Fly a kite
- Row a boat
- Ride a horse
- Support a notion
- Calculate a distance
- Get a manicure
- Allay a fear
- Ride a wave
- Hold onto an idea
- Lend a hand
- Create an environment
- Deposit a toll
- Predict a snowstorm
- Support a candidate
- Hit a bull's eye

★

How to Create a Buzz
About Your Bunkle

AS AN UNCLE, you'll find you must broaden your definition of bonding and your definition of first experiences. Bunkling can be an experience, a moment, an instant, a weekend, a juncture, or an achievement—planned or spontaneous. Despite what it is or where or how it happens, you've got to hype it as something special to the kids. You've got to create a "buzz" about your bunkle.

I've worked at two of the top ad agencies in the world. At one I learned the art of positioning, and at the other, the Unique Selling Proposition (USP).

Positioning is asking the consumer to think of your product in a special way among the jumble of seemingly similar products that clutter one's mind.

"Schaffer is the one beer to have when you're having more than one."

"You deserve a break today."

"We're number two; we try harder."

You learn nothing about product differences; they're simply uniquely "positioned."

Schaffer is for the beer drinkers that put away two six-packs a night (a good market for selling beer). McDonalds is more than a hamburger chain; it's a place that allows the hard-working women of America to relax. And Avis boasts of being in second place to appeal to the hard-working business people they service: they're always out to please and give a little extra to make the sale.

It's about how you present the idea, not about the product or service itself.

The USP had its roots in the early days of television, when every brand of toothpaste, soap, and underarm deodorant touted its differences to achieve its strategized piece of this new, extrasensory marketplace. The USP offers a demonstrable product difference, a "benefit" created by this difference, and a "reason why" the product will deliver its uniqueness.

"Helps build strong bodies twelve ways." Benefit? Strength. Reason why? Vitamin enriched.

"Melts in your mouth, not in your hands." Benefit? Chocolate without a mess. Reason why? A coated candy shell on the outside.

Positioning and USPs are two ways to present ideas; to persuade, convince, prevail on, or talk into. Since your job is to present whatever opportunity you have with your nephews and nieces as a "first," take the lessons of Madison Avenue to heart and apply them.

The USP Approach: Find a "First" and Describe Its Benefit

TO FIND A "FIRST," you've simply got to find things the kids haven't done before; the uniqueness of the activity will be apparent, and no matter what it is, it will seem special.

First speedboat ride. Benefit? Faster than you've ever traveled on the water before. Reason why? Motor moves boat quickly along the water.

First trip to a health club. Benefit? Be strong. Reason why? They've got all those iron-pumping machines.

First ride on a horse. Benefit? Be a real cowboy. Reason why? Cowboys use horses to take them across the terrain.

Do some research to determine which activities have yet to be covered by other family members. Look for things that you've always wanted to do, but never got the chance. Offer the benefit. Explain it. Then give the reason why.

Explore the fall foliage, make a pottery vase, walk across a bridge. But be careful. You might be surprised at what the kids have already done. Try to find something really new.

Positioning: Turn the Ordinary into the Extraordinary

POSITIONING DOESN'T REQUIRE you to actually do something the kids have never done before. You simply have to position an activity differently; not just your annual trek to Action Park, but "have you been on that brand-new, biggest, and scariest roller coaster of them all?" Dad has taken you to a baseball game, but "did you ever sit behind home plate?" Sure you've been to the lake, but "have you ever gone to the *north* shore"?

Turning the Ordinary into the Extraordinary

HAVE THEY:

- Driven in a car, but never hailed a cab?
- Crossed a bridge, but never gone through a tunnel?
- Gone to a zoo, but never an aquarium?
- Bicycled in the street, but never in the park?
- Ridden on a subway, but never used a Metrocard?
- Colored in a coloring book, but never saw the leaves turn during foliage season?
- Eaten an apple, but never picked one off a tree?
- Built a sandcastle, but never been to a construction site?

In order to determine whether to use USP or positioning, you've got to determine how ordinary or different your idea is. If it's mundane, it needs positioning. If it's interesting in its own right, it requires the benefit orientation of the USP.

Lester, a busy attorney at his own law firm, grabbed any opportunity he could to bunkle. One day his sister, who always encouraged him to take the kids out on his own schedule, asked for a favor. She needed to go for some medical tests on Wednesday and was wondering whether he would take care of Eli. Lester wanted to, but was working on a highly sensitive securities case and had unbreakable commitments at the office.

"I've been to your office," insisted Eli. "Can't we go bowling?"

"Go where your uncle takes you," demanded Mom, feeling a bit guilty at leaving Eli on a beautiful summer's day.

Lester did some quick positioning. There was a paper-shredding machine installed in his office for the new case. He repositioned it as a ferocious animal.

"I've got a hungry new pet in my office, with big sharp teeth that eats anything you put in front of it," coaxed Lester.

"Is it dangerous?"

"Not if you're careful."

The shredder lived up to Eli's expectations. It was the basis of a solid bunkle. Had Lester tried a USP approach, the conversation might have gone something like this:

"We've got a new piece of office equipment that you'll love. It automatically shreds up paper."

"What is it?"

"It's a paper shredder."

"What does shred mean?"

"It means tearing apart. Cutting it into little pieces."

"Why would you want to do that?"

"So that people won't be able to read what was written on it."

"Why not just throw it in the garbage?"

"Because someone might take it out of the garbage."

"Out of the garbage. Ugh. That's disgusting."

Positioning was the stronger approach. But, try pulling out your Swiss army knife and making a production of showing your nephew its built-in scissors, toothpick, screwdrivers, and pocket wrench. No need to position here. It is what it is, with obvious benefits and obvious reasons why. "Cool" is the response to expect. It's a good bunkle.

Take the kids to the supermarket at dawn and watch the workers unload the eggs. Treat them to a session of night court, bring them back stage at a show, or take them to the city dump. Drive them out to the airport and watch the planes take off and land. Go to the opera, or follow a fox back to his hole.

Actually, if you get good at this, you can secretly make a "first" work for you. "Who's never polished shoes so shiny that you can see your face in it?" "Who's never taken out the garbage in an apartment building?" "Who's never scratched somebody's back?"

Negotiate for some "firsts" with the parents. Can you take them to the zoo, bowling alley, batting range, or dance theater for the first time? Parents might happily share some of these pleasures. It's an uncle kind of thing to do. And a true "first," positioned or otherwise, is a bunkle that kids never forget.

Use Your Vocation To Bunkle

YOUR JOB MIGHT seem very ordinary to you, but it's probably fascinating to your nephews and nieces. From attorney to zookeeper, kids love to hear about the way you spend your day. Kids have already explored what Mommy and Daddy do, but as an uncle, you bring them further out of their sheltered world. A conversation, a trip to the office, a demonstration of a technique, or the sharing of a skill are all great ways to bunkle. By definition, many of these moments are actually "firsts." They can also enlighten, educate, and create the kind of shared event you are seeking.

While we were growing up, one of our neighbors was a retired dentist who was an eccentric recluse. He was not a friendly uncle, nor did he profess any love for children. But he was a magnet to kids. Every time Julian would pull his old, well-preserved 1949 Nash—a nearly extinct car at the time and surely impossible to find on the streets today—out of the garage and into the driveway, the neighborhood kids would gather round.

Julian, never Uncle Julian, would then do the strangest thing. He would selectively pull out some dental tools—usually a drill, a pick, a packet of filling materials, and gauze. He would then search for holes or tiny rust marks on the body of his car. Delicate dental procedures were performed on the troubled spots, and he would buff them to the smoothest of finishes, switching from drill to pick with agility, meticulously testing the perfection of his work as he must have done during countless root canals. We learned more about dentistry from Julian than from any book or visit to the dentist.

My uncle Jack used to take me to the family garment business. It was noisy and bustling with union labor, alarms to signify breaks, and giant spinning spools of thread. We would walk the floors together, supervising the many different workers: the shippers and cutters, the patternmakers and seamstresses. During breaks, my uncle would lift me onto the machine that traveled back and forth, laying down the fabric along the cutting table. I rode it like an amusement park ride, waving as I passed my uncle. The patternmakers and cutters had a good laugh.

"Jack's nephew," they would say. And we bunkled.

If you work in an office, have your niece or nephew do basic filing, letter stuffing, or photocopying. If you can't take them to work, bring them pictures, a souvenir, or a product.

Be expansive, not just factual. If you work in construction, tell them you build buildings. If you're a rocket scientist, say you help put men into outer space. If you're a farmer, say you grow the corn that goes into Corn Flakes. Make it all sound like you're answering questions about yourself, but remember that you're taking them into new worlds and broadening their horizons.

Then take it a little further. Start with the obvious questions and build from there. How do you build a building? What is a scientist? Who grows the cheers that go into Cheerios?

Move on to whatever level of sophistication the kids can handle. As you watch them grow, their questions will become more complex, and you'll soon find yourself talking to them about atmosphere entry points, the latest zoning restrictions on commercial properties, or how the drought in the Midwest will affect the federal government's tax increase.

Eugene was our second cousin, but due to age difference and attitude, he was more like an uncle. Each year, he'd come north to our home from Washington, D.C., for the family Passover Seder, and we'd pump him with the same questions about his job as a research psychologist for the Pentagon, over and over. What do you for a living? Is a psychologist a doctor?

As we grew older, the questions changed, but the subject remained the same: "Who is the Pentagon?" "What is an experimental psychologist?" "Why do they need you?"

With more education, I finally hit on something. I was about seventeen and had confronted Eugene with these questions annually since I was a kid. "You mean you decide when a pilot drops a bomb whether he should push or pull the lever?"

"Something like that," he smiled.

Share your war stories. Talk about commuting to work, your hours, your schedule, the characters you supervise or with whom you work, the legends of your industry, the glory of working for yourself. You don't have to pull out your latest IRS statement, but you can do a lot better than just saying, "I'm a lawyer."

Play show-and-tell. If you're a doctor, let them listen through your stethoscope. If you work as a carpenter, let them use your level. If you're a real estate broker, take them on a tour of an empty apartment. If you're an architect, show them how to build using Legos.

Take them out of the sheltered world constructed by their parents in some unique way. What seems everyday to you is probably extremely exciting to them.

★

Learn What Your
Nephews and Nieces Like To Do

IN THE 1970S, I mastered Ms. PacMan. I could hardly pass
a machine without dumping in a bunch of quarters. Although
Avi and Dani also indulged at the time, I was better than either
of them. There was a bond in our competition, a bunkle. And
although I am hardly as good at the new twenty-first century
video games as my younger nephews and nieces, I still try.
Bunkling is about sharing, not about winning.

Finding the things kids are into and showing an honest interest in those things is a wonderful bunkle. If they're interested in
baseball, pitch them a couple balls. Football? Toss the leather
around. Basketball? Play some one-on-one. Regardless of whether
you win or lose, the kids have an opportunity to show off their new
skills to their uncle. Be proud! That's what they want from you.

My nephew Dani became interested in photography as a
teenager and eventually made it his profession. I had always
used a simple "point and shoot" camera, but Dani motivated me
to get a new, more complex camera, study the manuals, and try
to understand the language of "f" stops, aperture openings,
backlighting, and fill flash. Photography has become an avocation of mine. It also stemmed from a bunkle.

Dani and I still meet and compare photographs and discuss lenses and what we see through them. Together, we uncover new things to shoot. He's found something he loves, and I can share it with him. I'm not nearly as good as he is, but I am probably as proud of his work as he is.

Bunkling Trips

TAKE YOUR NEPHEW or niece on a day trip and strengthen the bond. It need not be the obvious, like an amusement park, a zoo, or a ball game. And until they're much older, it should be just a day trip; no sleepovers. Pick a place or activity that you know the kids are old enough to enjoy. Taking a three-year-old to a health club makes no sense at all. Nor does taking a sixteen-year-old to the zoo. Look for the right ideas for the right kid and at the right age level. And try to be original. That's what uncles are about.

I like to think of these trips as experiences rather than travel. They can be a few hours' drive away or right next door, but I do stress that they should be something the kids have never witnessed or done before.

Consider taking them to a trade show. There's always one in town, like the gift show, the flower show, the stationery show, or the toy show. These are business events that can double as bunkling events. You may have to do some quick talking to get them in, especially the toy show, but your business card should generally be enough.

Let the children wander among the many stands operated by different suppliers of the trade, stop at those that feature a wide array of merchandise, tell them about commerce at its elementary best, and treat them to a hot dog alongside businessmen from around the world.

Or consider the many consumer shows. Let them sit in the driver's seat of the latest sports car at an auto show, fantasize about being on a desert island at a boat show, or let them lose themselves in cyberspace at a computer show.

Try a place they've never been to, like a batting range, bowling alley, or miniature golf course.

Introduce them to a new sport, such as billiards or boomerangs. Take them fishing, sailing, ballooning, or mountain climbing.

What about street markets, street fairs, rodeos, or tennis matches? Anywhere new, anything different.

Visit the main post office or the local fire station. Walk them through a tie store or a perfumery. Take them to the fish market and let them dump ice, to a cattle show to pick out Holsteins, to a truck stop to fill up with diesel, or to a biology lab to watch a frog dissection. Treat them to a shoeshine. Count coins at a Coinstar.

Leave the beach to the parents, unless you own a beach house; the outdoor art show for Mom or Dad, unless you have a prodigy. Avoid crowded theme parks, the usual tourist traps, and places with too much sun. Use your day trips to feed curiosities, usher in new worlds, and offer new experiences. Almost anything out of the ordinary is welcome to kids. They expect to escape with you, so let them, and enjoy!

Travel Tips

In the Car

1. Observe car safety rules. Use the appropriate car seat for infants and toddlers weighing up to forty pounds, and make certain it's properly positioned and secured.
2. Know how to get where you're going. Kids get impatient when you're lost, and so do you.
3. Prepare good car games in advance.
4. Consider scenic stops or places of interest along the way.
5. Learn where the bathrooms are as soon as you get to your destination.

Restaurant Pointers

1. Pick kid-friendly restaurants (food that comes out quickly, menus that caters to youngsters).
2. Look for space, not intimacy.
3. Look for noise, not quiet.
4. Avoid restaurants with cloth tablecloths.
5. Don't order anything that takes more than ten minutes to prepare.
6. Look for buffet-style restaurants.

Other Ways of Getting There that Kids Will Remember

- Railroad
- Bus (especially double decker)
- Ferries
- Subways
- Taxis
- An animal drawn cart
- Tunnels and bridges
- Elevators and escalators

UNCLEDOTE

⭐ Bunkling Without Being There ⭐

AT FOURTEEN, MY *niece Yonina, on her first solo trip to Manhattan, was immediately enamored by the tall prewar buildings, the beauty and constancy of the shops, the busy traffic with buses pulling in and out, and the people crossing every which way. She stared out the window of my sixteenth floor apartment, facing Broadway in awe.*

I put a pile of quarters on my kitchen table and made a deal with her. I drew a map of the west side of Manhattan on a napkin, showing where Broadway crisscrossed Amsterdam, the difference between the east side and west side of the street, how the numbered streets logically went up and down in order, and the location of some key shops and landmarks. The deal: She could walk the streets of the west side alone, but every fifteen minutes, she must make a phone call to me describing where she was.

We synchronized our watches.

"I'm in front of the Chase Manhattan bank," she called in dutifully. "In front of the Gap." "At the entrance of Fairway." "On Columbus and 75th Street."

Just before Yonina got married, she pulled something out of her top drawer to show me. It was the napkin on which I had drawn the map. She had saved it all these years.

Nicknames and Bunkling

BRANDING IS THE "buzz" on Madison Avenue today. Names are important, and a theory I subscribe to insists that the names be simple, meaningless sounds, related or unrelated to the product. They need not be descriptive. No basic concept is necessary, and no more than two syllables are required. Nicknames should be endearing and memorable; they should never be designed to hurt.

BEING A KID AGAIN

IN 1971 I was hit by a car, and my left leg was pretty badly injured. Surgical pins had to be inserted into my leg to hold the bones in place. It was summer time, and I was particularly blue about the prognosis: five days in the hospital, six weeks in a cast, crutches, physical therapy.

Late that night, my uncle Jack ducked into my hospital room long after visiting hours were over, all alone. Nothing could have cheered me up more.

Unk started to play. First the electric bed. "I want to take one of these home with me," he said. Then he placed the emergency oxygen mask over his face and rolled his eyes. He cranked the adjustable table up and down and up again. And finally, he discovered the nurses' call button.

"What's this?" he asked, knowing exactly what it was. He pushed the button. He had something up his sleeve.

When the night nurse arrived, she found my uncle lying on his belly—in ambush position—in the middle of the room, with one of my crutches poised like a rifle in his hands. Using the crutch's grip as the trigger and the rubber tip as a barrel, he stared down its imaginary site, aiming, ready for his prey. As the flabbergasted nurse stepped into the room, Unk did his famous machine gun imitation: "Ta ta ta ta ta ta ta."

Letting Go

THERE'S AN INTENSE need for control in most of our lives. Not only in the "do it my way" sense, but also in the subtle ways people regularly act to influence being liked and loved. When you give up some control, you remove the responsibility of being forced into a particular performance, and you no longer feel obligated to play guide or mentor. When spending time with your niece or nephew, you can escape from the daily demands of your environment, spend some precious, peaceful time untouched by the demands of dating, courtship, and marriage. You can be yourself; you can be an uncle.

I'm not proposing you become irresponsible. Heaven forbid, especially with kids. But I do suggest you give up some power in order to become a kid again. Adult control, after all, is a sore subject with kids. And at one point or another, you're going to be seen as one of them. Try this: On a day out with your nephews and nieces, do not suggest a place to go. Don't say miniature golf, the batting range, or the movies. Don't mention a day on your sailboat, a Sunday doubleheader, or a morning in the sandbox. Without making a suggestion, let your nephew or niece decide exactly what he or she would like to do. And unless it's dangerous or ridiculously expensive, agree to go along with it. It's likely you will end up at a water park or a bowling alley. Or perhaps even the Sunday doubleheader. But since the kids made the choice, you are ten steps ahead. You've relinquished power.

"I want the red ball. The red ball." "My turn, my turn!" "I need a hot dog."

That's you talking, not the kids. Because letting go of your need to control allows you to be a kid again.

"Cool." "Amazing." "Let's go on the waterslide again. And again. And again. Whee."

Work on being a kid again. You'll find that you'll get as much fun out of this relationship as they do.

You're an Uncle, Not a Parent: Relax

CHILD PSYCHOLOGISTS AND parenting experts have pinpointed average and expected behaviors by age. If used as general guidelines, these predictable behaviors can enhance your uncling experience, pave the way for opportunity, and offer insight into gift-giving, playful ideas, trips, and much more. Milestones will remind you of the kid you used to be, and they will help you get in touch with the kind of kid your nephews and nieces are today. But these average behaviors, if taken too seriously, can deter appropriate uncling by presenting obstacles and frustrating your expectations. Milestones, after all, cannot predict the future.

Imagine yourself as Albert Einstein's, Michael Jordan's, or Martha Stewart's uncle. Could you have used milestones to predict behavior? It's unlikely that Einstein squared equations on the potty, that Jordan jumped out of his crib at four months old, or that Martha Stewart emerged from the womb with the recipe for the perfect apple pie.

Reach out to your nephews and nieces as individuals; refuse to pigeonhole them. Recognize that each nephew and niece develops at his or her own pace, actualizing an individualized set of strengths and weaknesses, each at a different stage. Resist any developmental expectations you may have of your nieces and nephews. There are no hard and fast rules determining capabilities or faculties of any kid at any age.

Stages of Your Nephews' and Nieces' Lives

FROM THE TIME of birth to the toddler stage of a child, there's one important thing to remember: Don't let your inability to relate keep you away.

It's virtually impossible to remember yourself as an infant or as a toddler, learning to stand or walk. And while putting yourself in a kid's shoes is what this chapter is all about, you can, if you want, choose to sit back at this stage, watch them develop, and be as hands-off as you like.

Do, however, make some attempts at bonding; there's nothing like an infant's coo, cradle, or cuddle. There's fun in just tracking progress; when they begin to shake the rattle, stand on their own, sit up, eat solid foods, or take their first steps. Since you see the baby less often than the parents, you will be in a great position to notice change. A good uncle will marvel.

Under no circumstances, however, should you allow this seemingly passive uncling stage to go by unnoticed. Babies' personalities do start to emerge even at this early age and so will yours as an uncle. Are you a shy or an extroverted uncle? Are you singing lullabies, cradling them, and rocking them to sleep? Do you recognize their sounds or get reactions when you make faces? Do you baby-sit, diaper, and feed? Do as little or as much as you comfortable with, but don't wait for the child to grow up to be an uncle. Be an uncle from the beginning.

Now is also a good time to gauge the reactions of your extended family. Are they comfortable letting you play, or do they watch over you every second? Do they share in your delight, or are they burdened by concern? Build trust with them. Grab an uncling opportunity and run with it. Learn to support the baby's neck and back and hold him or her for a while. Mark the baby's first smile at you with celebration. Get down on the floor and supervise a crawl. Just pray the baby doesn't howl every time you get near.

Know this about toddlers: You'll never make sense of their demands, so don't even try. What separates toddlers most from infants is language. Now is the time they begin to speak and understand, if not complex sentences, certainly names of objects, parts of their body, their own needs, wants, and demands. They repeat commands, can follow instructions, and recognize bedtime stories. They can even say, "I love you."

The problem is that their thinking has not yet caught up with their speech. They will hear the words, be able to repeat them, and maybe even understand them, but they still might reflect an absolutely opposite emotional state or physical reality.

Toddlers magically believe that if they voice a request it must somehow come true, that adults are there merely to meet their needs. I want to be picked up. I want to be put down. Take me home. Let me stay. They throw temper tantrums, show disgust and disdain, disagree loudly and vehemently. They get upset easily.

Toddlers are among the most egocentric beings on earth. It is at this stage of growth that uncles start to be appreciated in their unique roles. While everybody else is always contradicting them, punishing or showing them a better way to do things, along comes uncle to do exactly what they want. Uncles give them piggyback rides, again and again and again. Uncles hand them the cookie they want, read the story they want, and let them stay up past their bedtime. You are now the good guy you always wanted to be. Of course, that's because you don't have to live with the kids; you just drop in for the occasional visit.

But be warned. You are no better at interpreting a two-year-old's logic or lack of it than anybody else. There is bound to come a time when your toddler nephew or niece gets upset with you. They might scream when you come near or suddenly turn on you and make Mom their ally. They might refuse to talk, play, or even look at you. This is but a little taste of what these brats have been giving their parents. There's no need to analyze or study their motivations; you probably won't get anywhere anyhow. Just observe one important rule: Don't take it personally, even if they say they hate you.

When your nephew or niece turns three or four, it's time for you to exercise your skills at becoming a kid again. Now you're an uncle to a real person, perhaps a very little person, but one with personality, language, the ability to think symbolically, new physical dexterity, and a strong sense of independence.

At this stage, kids push the limits of their newfound skills and want you to be impressed. They speed on their tricycles, eat with silverware, climb trees, and build big teetering castles that look ready to topple as they place another last block carefully on top.

While curiosity starts to become a motivating force, kids still want a careful mix of the old and familiar with their novel, first-time experiences. An amusement park would be well appreciated, but so would a push on the local swings. You might try orchestrating an afternoon of coloring, cutting, and pasting or venture down to the beach for a walk on the sand. But don't force a maiden voyage to your bachelor pad yet. Let your nephew or niece dictate how they'd like to spend the time. Their new independent thinking is what's most important to them.

Symbolic thinking—don't confuse this with reason or logic—allows your young nephews and nieces to relate to objects, experiences, and stories that are not right in front of them. They can talk about another place and time, something that happened at preschool or Grandma's, or about yesterday or tomorrow. The conversation becomes slightly more adult, and you should be ready to start developing your skills as a storyteller, book reader, and uncle.

There's something else about their thinking you should keep in mind. They have active imaginary lives. You are Daddy, and they are Mommy; you are the school bus driver, and they are the teacher; you are the checkout cashier, and they are the supermarket shopper. Play along. They are really into this stuff. And they believe it.

Also, there is something that's bothering your nephews and nieces at this stage. They are slightly annoyed and disappointed in their parents in one important way, and this offers an unusual uncling opportunity. Little by little, Mom and Dad are giving them less attention, less moment-to-moment assurance, and less stability. In many ways, the kids are thrilled about this, since independence is such an important goal. But they do miss having an adult around all the time to marvel as they discover and perform new and exciting tasks.

Uncles, with their sporadic, sometimes unexpected, and noncommittal visits, can give the kids all the attention they need.

Devote yourself fully. Do not divide your attention. Do not just supervise. Be the kid that they are, and you'll build the foundation for becoming their favorite relative for life.

A TODDLER'S SENSE OF TIME: NONEXISTENT

KIDS DON'T KNOW what you consider fast or slow, long or short. Watch them sign their name: You could write a book in that time. But take a trip to a toy store, and you'll see what lingering is all about. Be patient and careful. This is the age when they want you to watch, not help, as they do things at their own pace. But remember: This is also the age that they'll run into traffic to catch a ball.

☆

It isn't until they reach school age that your nephews and nieces will begin to appreciate exactly who you are. This is the age when kids separate from Mom, test out their newfound independence, and begin to experience the accompanying ambivalent feelings. Suddenly, they realize that Mom is hardly perfect; that she can't always control situations or make everything okay. Gone are the days of kissing boo-boos and wishing the rain away. Both boys and girls are likely to start moving closer to their fathers for a word of assurance or a big daddy hug. Though they begin to seek recognition of their progress from a new circle of friends, teachers, and neighbors, they still want Mom and Dad's attention, their closeness, and their cuddles.

Now is your time to shine as an uncle. Parents are busy dealing with their children's ambivalent feelings and often make the mistake of taking them personally. Kids are involved in an emotional tug-of-war, trying to decide whether they belong in the adult or child world, trying to figure where it is safer, where it is more fun. You can step in with the perfect blend, offering a friendly place to discuss their ambivalent adult feelings while allowing them to continue to act like children. For the length of your visit or phone call, they know exactly who they are and where they want to be—just a kid enjoying his uncle.

Give them space, and try to be the safe haven they are looking for. Be both a responsible adult and a curious, silly child. Fuel their egos by parading your imperfections. You are about to become one of the most cherished adults in their lives.

Beyond Simple Games

THERE'S ALWAYS ROOM for playful games. I personally have mastered the skill of putting a bottle cap in my eye, holding it in place with a strong squint, and briefly parading around as a freak of nature.

I can tell a joke, as long as I can remember it. But unlike my friend Norman, I usually can't. Norman can memorize any joke he hears and deliver it with a perfection from which only a

MILESTONES & MOMENTS

⇛ Becomes toilet trained	⇨ Pulls you to the bathroom to see
⇛ Enjoys pretend games	⇨ Pretends to be you
⇛ Has temper tantrums when frustrated	⇨ You're the only one who can calm him down
⇛ Learns a new word every day	⇨ Says "uncle" and gives you a hug
⇛ Imitates others	⇨ Imitates you
⇛ Climbs	⇨ You give your first piggy-back ride
⇛ Opens doors	⇨ Crawls into your bedroom
⇛ Scribbles	⇨ Creates a personal design just for you
⇛ First tooth	⇨ Bites your finger

drum roll following the punch line is missing. Norman is a pediatrician, so it's a handy skill.

Riddles irritate me because they bring more attention to the asker than the audience. I'm always the first one to say, "Okay, what's the answer?" I suppose kids do enjoy a good trick question, every now and then. My nephews and nieces eventually understand.

Yes, I encourage you to master as many funny faces and noises as possible and share them constantly. Being able to burp on command is marvelous.

They'll love your routines, and years later—at confirmation, graduation, or on their wedding night—you can shoot one off as they pass you walking down the aisle. When we least expected it, my uncle Jack would ghoulishly turn back his eyelids and pull his jacket over his head, scaring no one, but delighting us all.

The point is that these methods firmly place you in the dominant adult role. You're a comedian, a brain twister, a magician, or an impersonator. You're the entertainer, and the kids are your audience. Kids do enjoy an adult who tries to make them laugh. But the difference between acting like a kid again and acting like an adult trying entertain them is also the difference between being a good uncle and a great uncle.

I do cut up orange peels and put them in my mouth to create a Halloween smile. I can whistle loudly with any two fingers and create a wicked sound by using suction as I hit my elbow to my side. But uncles should strive for more than just a quick laugh. They should take kids to new horizons, and they should see those horizons through the eyes of a child, not an adult.

How To Think Like a Kid and Act Like an Uncle

ONE OF THE most delicious things about kids is their curiosity, and uncles can be a great resource for feeding a kid's inquisitive mind. Uncles, however, do not just tell all. They set their nephews and nieces up, fooling them into arriving at new conclusions on their own. Kids, after all, are always up for a challenge.

There are various kinds of set-ups. You can try and capitalize on information kids don't have. Take them to a fruit store during peach season and say, "Find me a Macintosh apple. You know, those red, juicy ones. Find me one of those."

Go to McDonald's and say, "Let's get some German fries with our burgers, this time. Let's order those delicious German fries."

When you're approaching a drawbridge, wonder aloud, "How do those tall, tall mastheads manage to fit under this low bridge? I don't get it."

Some uncles use information kids do know, but haven't had reason to apply yet. Ask them to name six brands of cereal. Four chocolate bars. Five stores in the mall. Three brands of gasoline.

These are not riddles. Riddles are used to show off, are often disappointing, and usually have a "gotcha" kind of solution.

They are not jokes, because they have no punch line. Uncling is not about being silly. Silly is a big red nose, a funny face across the dinner table, or asking where the ketchup is when it's right under your nose. Nor is it about showing off. Showing off says, "I know something you don't know."

What we're talking about is changing a kid's perception, giving them knowledge, offering motivations to observe, testing their memory, and offering challenges that require them to apply life experiences.

"How long would it take a plane to get to Boston? How about a train? A car? A jogger?"

Think like a kid. Push them to the limit. They've got the information; make them apply it.

"Watch. The bus is going to sneeze. Be careful."

"I'll bet there's going to be a lady waiting for me at that window," as you drive up to a bank teller.

Or, "How does the mechanic know that a car came in for gas if he has his head under the hood all the time?"

The key to succeeding is in the challenge and the setup. Your job is to constantly assess their level of knowledge, spark their curiosity with a challenge, and then help them achieve it. Waiting for them to ask questions is very un-unclelike. And just providing the information without a challenge is hardly an uncle's way of dealing with things. After all, who cares that there are no apples in the summer, or that there's an air brake on the bus, or that there's a wire that triggers a bell as a car pulls into the gas station?

Turn information into a game, making the question more important than the answer, and you will make learning fun instead of a chore. How does the conductor know when to close the subway car? Why are school buses painted yellow? How do the police know when you are speeding? Where do the stairs of an escalator go?

Never talk down to a kid in an attempt to make yourself understood. The trick is to actually become a kid, a kid in an adult's body. An uncle.

Name two animals that have stripes. Nine different fruits. Three avenues in Manhattan. Four airlines. A soup that has macaroni in it.

Stating the obvious is another game I play.

"You think there are any restaurants on this block?" I asked my nephew as we walked down West 46th Street, Manhattan's "Restaurant Row."

"Who uses more electricity? Us or these signs?" I continued as we walked through Times Square.

"Do you think anyone here knows how to ice-skate?" I wondered aloud as we passed Rockefeller Center.

"Would you say there are a lot of people on this corner?" as we crossed Fifth Avenue.

"Do you think there are any cars on this road?" as we waited in traffic on the West Side Highway.

Let the kids fall into your trap, unknowingly, unwittingly, like a fox that falls prey to a hunter's snare. Then teach them a lesson, something in life they have yet to observe. If you are original in your presentation, I guarantee it will be something they will never forget.

Put on a kid's glasses when you're with your nephews and nieces, glasses that color the world with innocence and naiveté. Then set up the sting.

Do I make a pest of myself? No way! Because if I'm thinking like a kid, I am a part of the game. The questions become as challenging to me as they are to them. In fact, sometimes the challenge is so real that I create one even I have trouble with. After all, how quickly could you name seven kinds of nuts?

Are these teases? Deceptions? Contemptible ruses? Certainly not. This is uncling—uncling at its very best.

THINGS YOU CAN USE TO SET KIDS UP

- ➥ Women's buttons are on the right and men's are on the left.
- ➥ Thunder always follows lightning.
- ➥ The moon waxes and wanes.
- ➥ The day after February 28th is sometimes February 29th.
- ➥ Stereos play different things out of different speakers.
- ➥ Helium makes your voice high.
- ➥ Thanksgiving is always on a Thursday.

UNCLEDOTE

Ah, Gullibility:
Three Uncle Set-ups

1. *I bunkled with my nephew on our first trip together into Manhattan, when we were in the elevator on the way up to my apartment. No, the elevator didn't get stuck between floors, nor did the cable snap and send us hurtling down the elevator shaft. That's not bunkling; that's simply a nightmare. What I did was set him up.*

I told him I had to stop at a friend's apartment on the thirteenth floor and asked him to push the appropriate button. His hands went up and down, back and forth, jumping from twelve to fourteen, fourteen to twelve, unable to find the number thirteen.

"There's no thirteen," he finally said, perplexed.

"That's impossible," I insisted. "C'mon. Push thirteen." His hands went back and forth.

Finally, I explained the superstition surrounding the number thirteen that began years ago, and why even to this day it is so difficult to sell an apartment on the thirteenth floor.

2. *Uncle Larry set up his eight-year-old nephew Cliff during a surprise trip to nowhere in his shiny red sports car. As they approached a red light at a heavy traffic intersection, Larry* switched into neutral and wagered: "I'll bet I can predict the exact moment the light will turn green."

While Cliff stared at the light, waiting for the moment of change, Larry focused on the other side of the light, the side directing traffic going the other way. When that side of the light turned red, Larry revved up his engine, snapped his finger at the light they were waiting for, and announced, "Now!"

The light changed as if on command. Larry shifted into first gear, effortlessly leading traffic through the intersection.

3. One Sunday, Uncle Benjy took his nephew Timmy to buy a dozen mixed rolls for brunch. On the way over, Benjy set up the sting.

"Do you know how many rolls there are in a dozen?" he asked.

His nephew answered with the assuredness of a second-grader. "Twelve," he said.

As they walked from the parked car to the store, Benjy asked his nephew to please make sure the lady behind the counter gave him the right number of rolls. "I don't want to be cheated," he said. The rolls were carefully placed in a large paper bag; sesame, poppy, salted, and plain. Little Timmy dutifully mouthed the numbers, and just as he thought he fulfilled his mission, a thirteenth roll was dropped in.

"Uncle Benjy," he whispered, perplexed, in his uncle's ear. "They gave us thirteen!"

How Personality Affects Your Uncling

ARE YOU LONELY, angry, or delirious? Are you stable, employable, or sick?

Do you cross at the green and not in between? Can you amuse or sing or do tricks?

Are you picky with clothes, does your job make you cry, do you smile whenever you may?

Do you fear the word "no," hate sunshine or snow? Must things always go just your way?

Need you always be liked, recover quickly from lows, do you go on when people say stop?

Is your office too high, do you fear the word fly, must your cereal have blueberries on top?

Do you step on each crack, dread who's walking behind, do you exercise, or turn to drink?

An uncle is first just a person, and a person is just how you think.

You can't pass judgment on a personality. It is neither good nor bad, right nor wrong. Personalities are simply who you are; a function of how you think. Your personality can make you dangerous, weird, or unusually lovable. Even quirky personalities can be endearing. Personality can bring people closer or scare them away. It can make you fun, inquisitive, entertaining, or careful. And it can help or prevent you from being the best uncle you can be.

How you think affects virtually everything—from your career choice, relationships, and the car you drive, to whether you make a baby laugh. Your thoughts play a key role in molding your personality; they shape your sense of style just as easily as they can prevent you from living a healthy life.

Simple needs can overwhelm you, controlling your thoughts, behavior, relationships, and moods. Some suffer the roadblocks in life more severely than others, innocently or purposefully allowing them to thwart their dreams. What's key is deciding whether and how your personality helps or hinders your goals, as a person and as an uncle.

★

Be Aware, Not on Guard

YOU NEED NOT hide your neuroses as much as Dad, nor watch your frustrations as much as Mom. You can, after all—unlike parents—be yourself and leave without dealing with the repercussions. But it might be wise to rein in your narcissism or tone down your histrionics when they affect your relationships with your siblings or nephews and nieces. Allow your personality to rule, but do stop every once in a while to assess who you've become as an uncle and how that affects those around you.

Are you too lazy or too shy? Too fearful of success or failure? Rigid, morbid, or manipulative? Or, are you upbeat and outgoing? Fun, stable, and self-assured? Do you take responsibility; do you share and trust? Are you loyal?

Do you insist on predictability, substituting cautious involvement for real joy? Are your "shoulds" making you feel guilty—"I should take them out," "I should tell better stories," "I should visit more often."

Do you take every little comment to heart, feeling insulted or upset when a three-year-old says he never wants to see you again or a nine-year-old mocks the way you field a ground ball?

Uncling is a relationship that lets you act out, encourages you to be yourself, and lets you be free. But as in a working or romantic relationship, some aspects of your personality can be detrimental to the participants, and sometimes, frighteningly destructive.

As long as your behavior does not get in the way of your uncling, you have nothing to worry about. But when aspects of your personality begin to cause problems, keep you from getting closer, or make it harder for you to cuddle or love, you should think about taking a long look at your neurotic side.

Twelve Personalities, Twelve Uncles

1. I pinched my new niece (by marriage) once too often. Believe me, it was meant to be loving and playful; her cheeks are deliciously tempting. But my aggressive uncling style, so appealing to my other nephews and nieces, scared her. She ran, shy and upset, and hid behind her mother's skirt. It took months of gentle flirting to win her back.

2. Uncle Billy stole his nephew's chocolate fudge sundae from right under his nose. He first tasted and savored it teasingly, and then downed the entire dish of ice cream, cherry and all. He thought he was being cute. His nephew, however, thought he was mean and went crying to Mom bitterly and accusingly, seeing no humor in the situation at all.

3. Uncle Chris bonded easily with his nephew Phil. But he did it by offering him beer and cigarettes on their first fishing trip to the Delaware River and letting Phil take the wheel in the parking lot at the site of the old baseball stadium. Phil was nine.

4. Uncle Ted would accompany his nephew, Jim, on long walks through Jim's suburban town and discuss the important issues facing Jim's life. He was a great sounding board, a good listener, a favorite uncle. As Ted evoked his philosophy that ultimately things turn out for the better, he made sure to touch his foot on every crack along the way.

5. Ask Uncle Steve to spend a quiet afternoon alone with his nephew and he'll show up, but reluctantly. No shooting baskets or play dates with your friends, please. And no exotic trips to the shopping mall or the pizza shop either. Who might catch him in the act of uncling, pushing a swing, or missing a basket is crucial in Steve's mind. Steve is afraid of being judged. He fears being exposed as inept, and he sticks to doing the things he knows.

6. Uncle George dripped with charisma. A dapper sports agent, he'd mesmerize his two nieces with "tales from the real world," dropping the names of celebrities and turning tiny conversations into grandiose ideas. At an unexpected moment, he would charmingly whisk his nieces around the living room with perfect rhythm and timing. But if you criticized him about anything—like the way he dressed, how he combed his hair, or why he forgot to call you for your birthday—he would erupt into an uncontrollable rage, hurling hurtful comments designed to push sensitive personal buttons.

7. When Uncle Ben gets an invitation to take the kids out to Amusement Land, he immediately suspects he is being used. They don't really want me to be with the kids, he thinks, they probably have no one to take care of them. When he arrives, Mom and Dad announce they are coming along. Ben immediately suspects they want him to pay for everything. When they offer to pay, he is puzzled. They probably want me to take the kids back home while they go see a movie.

8. Uncle Carl prefers to be called just plain Carl. But that hardly matters since he's almost never around. Even at Thanksgiving dinner, when Grandma, Grandpa, and all the cousins gather together, Carl does not show up. He needs his space, he claims, pushing away even his nephews and nieces. No, he doesn't see that being an uncle is an important relationship or that any other relationship is important, for that matter. Yes, he would like to be left alone.

9. Uncle Lenny is a charmer; the kids look forward to his visits. But for some reason, Mom and Dad don't share the excitement. Mom never lets the kids go out alone with him, and his visits usually end in a family argument, often about money. Once he borrowed Dad's car and was in a small accident. Dad exploded and blamed him, assuming it was his fault, and declared him irresponsible. But Lenny always comes back, smiles and all, to see the kids.

10. It's hard to get close to Uncle Dick. On the one hand he's aloof and somewhat despondent, actually expressing his strong belief that he could never be the kind of uncle the kids deserve. On the other hand, he often peeks into the kids' rooms, hoping they will notice him and how much he really wants to be with them. But when they do finally approach him, he won't leave them alone for a second, demanding every moment of their attention. When he can't get that, he goes back to feeling unworthy.

11. Uncle Louie enters the house like a whirlwind. He declares he can only stay for a little while, orders a cup of coffee, and flops back onto that comfortable chair with the overstuffed pillows. He seems glad to see everybody, but at the same time, he doesn't appear to see anyone as an individual. He mesmerizes the kids, along with the adults, and if he loses their attention, he demands it back. Louie leaves as quickly as he arrives, blowing a kiss to the room.

12. Uncle Eddy finally decides to take his nephew to the zoo for a day, but it takes the longest time before they finally leave. There are so many things to decide, like which zoo they should go to? Should they take the car or public transportation? What about lunch? Should they pack it or buy it on the road? If they can't see the whole zoo, should they concentrate on inside or outdoor animals? Should he buy popcorn or pizza? Will his coat be warm enough?

Could Your Actions Hurt the Kids?

IT WILL NOT be the end of the world if you aren't the perfect uncle. It will not be awful if you make a mistake. Recognize that you must take risks to do better and that there is no such thing as failure, especially for an uncle who tries. Even if you can't play the piano, tinker on the keyboard. If you can't hold a bat, so what? Get out there on home plate anyway. If you can't sing, try it anyway, but at the top of your lungs. There are, after all, few perfect uncles in this world, and those who are might just be the nuttiest of us all.

Stepping on cracks doesn't hurt anybody; it can actually be rather endearing. Staying at home with your nieces and nephews, day after day, could get boring; if not for you, for them. And there's a very fine line between being right and being abusive.

UNHEALTHY EXCUSES
FOR NOT BEING A GOOD UNCLE

- ● I don't like children.
- ● It's sissy-like.
- ● They've got fathers.
- ● They've got aunts.
- ● It reminds me that I'm not married.
- ● I do not need any additional responsibility.
- ● I'm busy.
- ● I will embarrass myself.
- ● I never had a good uncle. Why should they?
- ● Kids are messy.
- ● My relationships never work out.
- ● I have kids of my own.
- ● Why me? I'm not good at anything.

Like millions of others, uncles suffer from neurotic thinking. They feel the need to control, to prevent bad things from happening to themselves, to their nephews and nieces, even to the rest of the world. If you can't make decisions, your nephews and nieces will love you anyway. And I suppose Uncle Louie, with his "here today, gone tomorrow" lifestyle that never allows anyone to get close, is still a whole lot of fun to be around. But no matter how charming, irresponsibility must be kept in check. The lives of the children are at stake.

My rule: Be as neurotic as the next guy. If you're withdrawn and reserved at work, forget your worries when you start to uncle. If you're attention-seeking on the dance floor, stifle the histrionics and just be yourself with your nephews and nieces. But when your actions start to get in the way of meeting your own goals—or worse, when they begin to turn you into an irresponsible adult—that's the time to do something about it.

Uncle Stereotypes:
Quirks, Icons, and Idiosyncrasies

NO ONE TRAIT affects your whole personality. Thank God. But in the uncle relationship—so loving, yet so sporadic—individual personality quirks often do emerge. Don't be surprised or upset when the kids start labeling you. Uncles are notorious for being loved, imperfections and all. The names are usually fair descriptions of who you are. Just keep your style in check and recognize when your issues start getting in the way: While it's fun to be called Uncle Tease, you don't want to be called Uncle Mean.

Here are some labels that kids can come up with for their uncles, based on their dominant personality traits; traits that can make you memorable, lovable, and annoying all at the same time:

- **Uncle Win! Win! Win!:** From basketball to Candyland, you must win! Why? Because winning defines you; it dictates who you are. Not your charm, your love, or your devotion, but winning. After all, nobody likes a loser. Let me roll the dice again, one of them fell off the board. Out of bounds! Out of bounds! Do over, do over! Stop worrying. Let your nieces and nephews win once in a while. To them, you'll never be a loser. You are their uncle.

- **Uncle Brood:** If you find yourself never having as good a time with the kids as you'd like—forcing yourself to go for visits, losing sleep over the way you treated them—investigate the possibility that you're suffering from depression. There are excellent medical and therapeutic treatments available today to help you overcome your melancholy. But remember, although it may be hard for you to believe, your nephews and nieces might not be seeing your moods; they love you just the way you are. Don't allow your own perceptions of yourself as a person or an uncle to get in the way of relating to the kids. Work on yourself, but never stop being an uncle. It could well be the very relationship that helps pull you through your crisis.

- **Uncle Tease:** Little Jackie is throwing the perfect temper tantrum; tears, screaming, and all. Nobody even remembers what the issue is anymore, and Mom, rightfully so, exercises a time-out—that new-fangled version of a spanking. It works. Finally she quiets down, wipes away her tears, and rejoins the real world. About ten seconds later, Uncle Neil pulls at her ponytail. The tantrum starts all over again. Yes, Uncle Tease, you can make a kid cry, get upset, stomp her feet whenever you want. But why not look for the laugh buttons as well; the buttons that will bring joy and a smile, that will light up her face and make both of you happy.

➻ **Uncle Instigator:** If your nephew and niece drop food on the carpet, you point out how permanent the stain is. If they steal a cookie out of the jar, you're the first to realize it's missing. You like to provoke, incite, and egg on. Unlike Uncle Tease, you're trying to get a rise out of your siblings, not just your nephews and nieces. Is your need to act out really worth it? Can't you just forgive and forget? Get over it!

➻ **Father-in-training:** You might avoid intimate relationships, refuse to commit to anyone for more than a week, and turn down blind dates because you might actually like them, but you do long to be a father. You diaper, burp, and baby-sit. You lecture, teach, and demonstrate. You teach, you offer an allowance, and insist upon bedtime. Lighten up: Don't use these kids to fulfill your own needs. Toss them around a bit, tease and tickle them. Break the rules sometimes. Just as you need to be a father, they need to be nephews and nieces.

- **Uncle Natty:** You dress to perfection; have an outfit for virtually any uncling activity. You pick lint off shoulders and brush dust off laps. You love your nephews and nieces, but wish they wouldn't be so damn messy. Jump in, Uncle Nat. Throw a diaper over your shoulder and take a risk. Tuck your designer tie into your shirt, put on a bib, and get dirty. Don't put off bonding until the kids are as neat and clean as you are. It might never happen.

- **Uncle History:** You live in the past and love to tell stories of times gone by; what Mom was like as a teenager, how Grandma got angry with you when you wrecked the family car, the way you felt when they impeached Richard Nixon. Yes, you do play an important role in connecting the kids to something bigger. But try spending some time in the "here and now." After all, you weren't an uncle back then. You are an uncle today.

- **Uncle Old Fart:** You never want to do anything; you won't play catch, go out for a hamburger, or even get off the couch, so they can forget about a trip to the State Fair. But the kids seem happy to see you, and you do swing them into the air when you first arrive. You even bring them toys and gifts. Kids need different kinds of attention from their uncles, attention that goes beyond what they get from Mom and Dad. This has nothing to do with age, just attitude. Get over it.

- **Uncle Tightwad:** So the rainbow sprinkles cost five cents more. They've shrunk down the size of a chocolate candy bar, and it's hardly worth buying anymore. Arcades just eat up quarters. It's cheaper to rent a movie than go out to the theater. You buy them a gift because it was on sale at the ninety-nine-cent store. You're willing to take them to the museum, but only on Tuesday when it's free. C'mon, Uncle Tight. Life is short. Be a sport. Be an uncle.

- **Uncle Procrastinator:** You promise a trip to a zoo. It never happens. You swear you're going to bring them back a gift from Tahiti. You forget. You say you'll e-mail them once a week, you don't. We know this isn't malicious. But do the kids know? You could become Uncle Disappointment if you keep it up.

- **Uncle Righteous:** You think their skirts are too short, their hair is too long, and they should be reading books instead of watching television. Kids hate this stuff. They get enough of it from Mom and Dad. And you're not so perfect either. Give the kids a break. Be an uncle, not a father.

- **Uncle Military:** You can't order them around. You're not their lieutenant. My God, you're not even their Dad. Yes, they respect you as an adult. But this business of "children should be seen and not heard" has not been around since World War II. They will obey any reasonable request; get you a fresh glass of water and promptly throw away your wet napkin. But they will refuse to say, "Yes, sir!" "Yes, uncle" will have to do.

- **Uncle Know-It-All:** You know everything and you have no problem telling anyone, even if they didn't ask. From the presidential election to the weather, you know exactly what's going to happen. Although most of what you have to say is not fact but opinion, it's your presentation that makes you unique. You exude omnipotence. And when you're wrong, which invariably you are, you always have an excuse. It's hard to love someone so predictable, but we do. Try saying "I don't know" every once in a while. It will do wonders in getting you the love you want.

- **Uncle Show-Off:** Watch me make a rabbit appear out of a hat. Watch me find the king of hearts. Watch me make three out of three baskets. Watch me say the ABC's backwards. We get it. You want their attention. But isn't it supposed to be the other way around?

- **Uncle Doormat:** You get them what they want, when they want it, and how they want it. You never allow them any normal frustration, quaking with fear they might reject you. "Climb every mountain, ford every stream" is more than a lyric from *The Sound of Music*. It's your motto, your mission. It's how you connect to your nephews and nieces. Watch out. You can get hurt here. They might think they're entitled to this type of treatment and start treating you like their servant instead of their uncle.

- **The Creep:** You wear thick glasses and don't attract women. You babble rather than talk, often forget to shower, and your gifts are way off base. You're weird. But the kids welcome you; they even need you. You might not be what they want for themselves; you might not even be what you want for yourself. But you are their mom's brother, and that makes all the difference.

- **The Pleaser:** You do magic tricks, card tricks, practical jokes, and funny faces. There's never a moment of silence around you. You're always telling a joke, singing a song, or trying to get them to laugh. Even the kids know you give them too much money, too often. And they wish you'd let them please you once in a while. Unk, take a break. They'll love you anyway.

- **Third-Date Louie:** They've figured out your M.O., Unk. You bring dates with you to baby-sit, and if they last three dates at home with the kids, you figure they're good mommy material. Louie, look for a woman, not a mommy. Now that they know your game, they're going to decide in advance just how good a time your second baby-sitting date will be.

UNCLEDOTE

Fearless, But Afraid

LUTHER, A COLLEGE *football star with a physique to match, was excited about becoming an uncle. Hearty back-slapping, tossing the ball around in the backyard, jogging side by side along the river, even fishing were his visions if the baby were to be a boy. Going out to the mall, showing her off to his friends, and charming her on the dance floor were his visions if it turned out to be a girl.*

When the baby finally arrived, the family gathered at the hospital, passing the infant boy from Grandma to Grandpa and from sibling to sibling. Uncle Luther sheepishly stood off to the side of the room, busying himself with the camera, positioning himself as the family photographer. Finally, the baby was offered to him. He refused. Like the football cheers that so energized him on the field, everyone began to egg him on. "C'mon Luther. Take the baby. C'mon." Luther was afraid, fearful that his inexperience would show—that perhaps he would hold him wrong or maybe even drop him.

Some Serious Words About Tickling

Fact of Life

PEOPLE WITH EASY access and those who are familiar to their victims form the great majority of child molesters. Uncles are therefore often suspects. Tickle as much as you want, but underarms and foot bottoms only, please. And when the kids cry "uncle," comply. There's a point where tickling becomes torture and you never want to go there.

Healthy Reasons To Uncle

- ➜ I love being around kids.
- ➜ I want to mentor.
- ➜ I need family in my life.
- ➜ It fulfills a responsibility.
- ➜ It gets me closer to my siblings.
- ➜ I have something to offer.

WHAT THE FAMILY
WANTS FROM YOU

Mothers mother. Teachers teach.
Police police. Judges judge.
And uncles? They uncle. And thank God for that.

IMAGINE IF SUDDENLY there was an uncle slowdown—a refusal to swing kids high into the sky before you took off your coat and no more pinches on the cheek or post-bedtime phone calls; no more fish caught, visits to the monkey house, kites flown, or mountains climbed.

Now go to the other extreme and imagine a sudden surge in uncling. Too many dinners interrupted, weekends spent in pure joy and fun, bedtime horror stories told, magic tricks performed, unusual sounds produced, and distorted faces made.

A move toward definitions and family expectations of uncles would be a perfect step forward. You would still be able to choose to uncle or not, just as you can reject the assigned roles of marriage or religion. But at least the choice would be a clear-cut and informed decision, with no confusion about your obligations or responsibilities.

The Perfect Uncle

WE EXPECT YOU to be a model to kids, often filling voids of behavior not experienced at home; yet we expect that uncles will not interfere with the parents' child-raising,

You can be spontaneous in your contact; you need not operate on a clock. But when you're with your nephews and nieces, you are expected to adhere to normal adult rules of responsibility and exhibit trust, loyalty, consistency, and reliability.

You put smiles on kids' faces. On a particularly sad or rainy day, there's nothing like having you over or going to your house. But keep your fun good and clean, and never expose the kids to danger, offensive language, or shady activity.

You are a negotiator, a King Solomon-like character who is able to see differences objectively, between parents and kids and nephews and nieces. You carefully weigh the possibilities of rapprochement, often having private conversations on both sides, never scolding or trying to control the situation, never taking a side.

You have no rules for gift-giving; no rules about cost or suitability, good sense or practicality. Your gifts are like your visits: erratic, spontaneous, and memorable.

Perfection Doesn't Make You an Uncle; Family Does

ALTHOUGH FEW FAMILIES live up to society's expectations, the family has had institutionalized goals for thousands of years. Family helps society produce the next generation, regulate sexual behavior, protect children, and provide comfort for adults, and help parents focus on work.

Of course, every family differs in structure and lifestyle. In America, about half of all marriages are remarriages, and nearly twenty percent of all children live with stepparents. There are single-parent families, absentee-parent families, a growing number of gay families, and families where children are shuttled back and forth between parents. There are orphans with no family at all.

America emphasizes the importance of the nuclear family, but we can hardly ignore the extended family. Relatives—even those not living in the same state, region, or country—often play a significant role in our lives. They visit, write letters, and make telephone calls. E-mail and the Internet have proven to be incredible boons for the extended family.

Take Grandma and Grandpa. Major advances in the field of medicine allow them to live longer lives and have far more active lifestyles, which has led to new definitions of their roles. A number of states have actually enacted or introduced grandparents' rights legislation, allowing seniors to fight for custody of their grandchildren. More and more books have been published, both academic and anecdotal, about the role of the grandmother.

But what is the role of the uncle? Your skills, shortcomings, and persuasions do not define your unclehood. No matter how crude you are, you're still an uncle. Why? What defines you is how you shape and affect society, both positively and negatively, through an established societal institution; supporting its ideas, its goals, and its reason for existing.

How do you uncle? That's like asking how you mother. Mothers nurture. Uncles encourage. And they accomplish this by offering adult companionship to kids that is different from the more controlling adult relationships they are used to.

If you make even the most unpolished or gross attempt at keeping your nieces and nephews happy—if you offer even the bare minimum amount of validation, motivate only momentary—you'll not provide long-term joy, but you're still playing your role. You are unique in a child's life. You are an adult, you are a friend, you are family.

That's why just making a kid laugh is good uncling.

Like loving mothers who drive recklessly and supportive fathers who drink two six-packs a night, you can be an endearing uncle even if you yell and scream, consistently take sides, and make children cry as soon as you get near. You can offer your nephew his taste of wine or taste of brew or your niece her first tube of red lipstick. You can arrive empty-handed on Christmas, never call before coming over, and make them swing a bat again and again until they get it right.

Even negative models can sometimes work. Eat like a slob at the table, and your nephews and nieces might button up their manners. Be loud and boisterous, and they might finally understand what quieting down is about. Put your feet up on the couch, and you might hear, "Mommy says we can't do that."

A particularly doting uncle I know was the source of *Playboy* magazines for his nephews in summer camp. In his mind he was encouraging them to be men and introducing himself as a safe haven from the challenges of co-ed sleep-away camp. Sure, he was unappreciated by the head counselor and parents, and he should have thought twice about his behavior. But he was being an uncle; an uncle in the truest sense of the word.

★

On Being a Gay Uncle

FOR GAY MEN, being an uncle can be even more important and more meaningful a relationship than for most men. Uncling may be your closest contact to children and especially if you love little kids, this can fill an important void.

There are two different kinds of gay uncles: Those who are accepted by their families and those who are not.

If you are accepted, you will be an uncle as welcome as any. If you're single, you are less likely to have any immediate issues, but if you're in a committed relationship, you should talk to your siblings and in-laws about the particulars of your relationship. Should you discuss your sexuality with your nieces and nephews or leave it to the parents? At what age will the kids understand the difference between gay and straight? What, if anything, do the kids understand already? Can you bring your boyfriend over to baby-sit? Your blind date? Can you take the kids to gay events—a gay pride parade, for instance? If you decide to have kids yourself, will they be accepted as cousins?

If you are not accepted, your problems are not unlike other uncles who, for whatever reason, have been shunned by the family. When you do get together on those rare occasions, approach your nephews and nieces carefully, but lovingly. It will be slow work to gain their trust and the trust of your siblings. Immediately swinging them high into the air could be inappropriate. The kids might be pulled away from you even for an innocent response on their part or yours. Send them birthday and

Christmas cards and unexpected gifts, even if you don't see them often. Your goal is to keep the uncle relationship alive in the minds of the kids.

Keep in mind that growing up, your nephews and nieces most likely won't immediately understand that you're gay, even if it's explained to them. When they become adults, they will be able to appreciate you for who you are. Do all the things uncles do, adding your own special personality, quirks, and creative energy. After all, you're hardly a gay uncle, nor are other uncles straight uncles. You are just an uncle, a kid's favorite relative.

★

Role Conflicts

BESIDES BEING UNCLES, we are citizens, deacons, fathers, and teachers. Sometimes, life can make it difficult to uncle, to be loyal and present for the kids, to be consistent and trustworthy, or to be there at all. Is it an uncle's job to straighten out kids? Must he perform if obstacles are thrown in his way?

Divorce, for example, can wreak havoc on families, and uncles invariably get caught in the middle. Coming out of the closet can cause conflict. So can being "born again." Even being a father to your own children can get in the way of good uncling. Geography, unshared values, and life's predictable and unexpected crises can all damage a cherished relationship. What's an uncle to do? Do what a divorced mom, a grieving widow, or a young divorcee would do. Start over. Examine your uncle opportunities, rethink your expectations, and jump in. You'll make mistakes; everybody does. But that too is a part of being an uncle.

HELP SOLVE THESE UNCLE CRISES

1. Two years ago, Jamie divorced his wife and lost custody of their three children. At first, he got together with his kids once a week. Jamie's brother, Uncle Ted, who was a second father to the kids, often came along on these visits. But then, Jamie met an attractive out-of-towner, married her, moved to Florida, and adopted her little girl. His kids were to come down south for part of the holiday season and during their summer vacation. What's going to happen to Uncle Ted's relationship with his kids?

2. Uncle Sid lives in St. Louis. His three nieces live in Atlanta. Neither he nor his brother have the money nor the inclination to travel much. They were close as kids and remain close through the telephone contact they have, but Sid, who has no children, wants to know his nieces better. What's a long-distance uncle to do?

3. My dear friend Alan suffered a tragedy as an uncle. His sister and brother-in-law were killed in a fire leaving behind two heartbroken teenagers. Alan ran a strictly observant Jewish household, complete with ritual and religion, a lifestyle his late sister and brother-in-law expressly did not wish for their children. A single, never-married aunt offered to bring up the kids. What's Alan to do?

General and Specific Uncling Skills

AS WITH ANY other role, what separates one uncle from another is, ultimately, performance. Which skills are used, their quality and frequency, and the extent to which they fulfill expectations are all important.

Take cops. Their role is to police. Within that role, various hats can be worn: Traffic manager, detective, patrolman, photographer, fingerprinter. And a variety of personal skills are employed: diplomacy, marksmanship, psychology.

That's why all cops are not the same. Each performs his role differently. Some are better, some are worse, but no two are the same.

Reading X-rays doesn't make you a doctor. Nor does writing on a blackboard make you a teacher. An excellent art director might not know how to draw, and some of my favorite teachers never learned my name. Are you unworthy as an uncle if you can't do magic tricks or if your gifts are corny and unusable?

Uncles too wear many hats. Clown, tutor, and baby-sitter. Chauffeur, chess partner, and horsey. Driving instructor, gift-giver, and movie partner. Like cops, these hats are only performance aspects of the role, not a description of the role itself. Some hats fit better than others, and you may live up to some expectations but not others and still be considered an uncle.

But there are expectations. We expect that doctors will wear a white coat during an examination; that teachers will give homework; that children won't drink alcohol. You need not be multiskilled, perfectly adept, or even an expert in any particular area, in order to be a fine, well-respected role player. As long as your performance—as an uncle, teacher, cop, or otherwise—moves toward accomplishing the goals of your position, you are playing that role. Just put a smile on your nephew or niece's face, and you can collect your paycheck at the end of the week.

Of course, as role expectations get more specific, your role performance becomes more demanding. Ophthalmologists had better know how light affects the cornea. English teachers sure better know how to spell. And if you're a fingerprint expert, you'd better learn to use a computer or you'll be back walking a beat.

As society changes, so do roles. HIV and AIDS pushed immunologists to the forefront; personal computers did the same for computer teachers.

Uncles too are varied in their performance. Like a doctor who decides to specialize in psychiatry, an uncle can specialize in weekends at his country home. Like a lawyer who decides to chase ambulances, an uncle can decide to coach a baseball team. Like teachers who choose to specialize in history or civil servants who work in sanitation, uncles can choose the way they uncle.

Burp, kiss, push a swing. Tell a good story, buy a great gift, send flowers or chocolate. Take trips to the library, the museum, the beach, or night court. Sleep over or sleep in. Toss around a football or swing around a nephew. Sing a lullaby or shout a cheer. Make a kid smile or stop a kid from crying.

Whether you stand on your head while yelling a Bronx cheer or help a kid discover the Big Dipper on a dark night under the stars, as long as it's encouraging, as long as it works to extend the family and build self-esteem, it doesn't matter what you do—you are an uncle.

When your nephew confides in you about his first girlfriend, when your niece meets you for weekly dance lessons, when your two-year-old nephew will make a doo-doo on the potty, but only if Uncle Marty takes him, you know your skills—personal and practical—are being put to use.

But like doctors, teachers, and civil servants, the specific expectations of an uncle change with the circumstances. Your extended family, its myriad of relationships and egos and its own dynamics at its nuclear center will all affect your role expectations.

After all, you probably won't do much bowling if Dad belongs to a father/son bowling league. And if Mom won't let her kids out of her sight, you won't be taking then on a picnic in the mountains. On the other hand, if your brother-in-law hates sports, your sister won't buy popcorn at the movies, or neither parent can shake, rattle, and roll—you've got opportunities.

SOME UNCLE HATS,
AND TIPS ON WEARING THEM

EDUCATOR	Teach, don't preach.
FAMILY HISTORIAN	Draw a family tree with an uncle on top.
SAFE HAVEN	Consistency and loyalty—that's what counts.
ADULT SIBLING	Gift certificates for "one night's baby-sitting." Three weeks' notice please.
CONFIDANT	Share your most embarrassing moment with your nephews or niece. Edit as necessary.
STORY TELLER	Tell the kids, if you can, exactly where you were the moment you heard they were born. They'll love it.
FRIEND	Take the kids somewhere you want to go.
GRANDPA'S SON	We know the kids like you better than Grandpa, but give your Dad his respect.
MORAL GUIDE	Model, don't preach.
MEDIATOR	Never have the final say.
NEGOTIATOR	Better than mediating.
FUTURE FATHER	No favorites!
SUBSTITUTE FATHER	You're close, but you can never be the real thing.
GIFT-GIVER	Forget price; be creative.
CONFIRMER OF IDENTITY	Never judge.
CHAUFFEUR	Car seats and seat belts, please. It's the law.
CLOWN	Try it in front of a mirror first.
TEASE	Don't do unto others what you wouldn't want done to you.
PHOTOGRAPHER	Make sure there's film in the camera.

UNCLEDOTE

KATHY HAD VERY *definite ideas about how she wanted to celebrate her ninth birthday. "My friends only," she said. Which was fine with the adults who could happily live without a noisy day at Funland. When the big day came, Kathy was in tears.*

"Where's Uncle Lenny?" she cried.

"You said you only wanted your friends," her mother said.

"But Uncle Lenny is my friend, Mommy," Kathy insisted.

★

How To Give Gifts

KIDS LOVE GIFTS, especially from their uncles. A gift from you means that you thought of them since your last visit. Although an uncle's gifts need not be more appropriate than anyone else's, nor is it mandatory or expected at each visit, gifts can be bonding, especially when timed to coincide with special moments in a child's life.

Determine what's going on with your nephew or niece so that your gift works to recognize the moments that matter most. If they've just learned to ride a bike, buy them a top-of-the-line bike horn or biking gloves (the kind the pros wear come in kids sizes). If they've just started school, get them something unexpected from the stationery store. Involve them in a conversation about coin collecting and if they seem interested, give them a starting set. Take them to the planetarium and buy them a telescope.

For annual events, try getting them something they want. But don't ask or pull the information out of them. What I do is surmise a good gift from conversations and activities I share with them. An interest in how things are made can result in an appropriate encyclopedia or CD. The same goes for an interest in botany, baseball, or banking.

Ten Tips on Taking Better Photographs of Your Nephews and Nieces

1. Keep your camera ready.

2. Get close.

3. Keep your nephews and nieces busy.

4. Use simple backgrounds.

5. Place your nephew or niece off center.

6. Include foreground in scenic shots.

7. Look for good lighting.

8. Hold your camera steady.

9. Use flash when necessary.

10. Choose the right film.

Sometimes, I admit, I walk the floors of retail stores. That's a difficult way to go, quite time-consuming, often frustrating, but a valid approach that can yield good results. A light will go off in a men's clothing store—a money clip! Something will click in a fancy food store—a collection of jams and jellies. A friend once had a brainstorm in a stationery store—he ordered personalized, informal cards for his nine-year-old niece.

At rites of passage, I tend to get misty. I buy gifts that will last and be remembered. Leatherbound or frilly things, silver or gold commemorative objects; anything that can be engraved. You can buy spoons, leather boxes, diaries, or jewelry.

Personal items always make great gifts, especially objects that have been in the family for years—Grandpa's old letter opener, his stamp collection, or his favorite fountain pen. You validate your role as generation-connector, as well as gift-giver.

Or give personal items of your own. An old bowling trophy, a well-used, broken-in wallet, or a football from the back of your closet. In my college days, I was a licensed basketball referee. Our whistles were far superior, louder, shrieker, and certainly cooler than the whistle an average kid owns. I wrapped one up and offered it as a gift.

Bring tacky souvenirs from business trips and vacations. Start a shot glass collection or a city map collection. Send them postcards. Think of them while you're away. Preserve their work; laminate a composition, frame a work of finger-painting art.

Try giving them something you've created—woodwork, a short story, a painting, or a model sailboat.

Where to shop? I use catalogs to peruse and the Internet to do research. I walk through retail and department stores searching for inspiration. I love flea markets and street fairs. I've bought antique trading cars and bubble gum machines. You never know where the light bulb will go off. I look for kids' gifts everywhere: in furniture catalogs, bathroom departments, and housewares sections. I walk through hardware stores and drug-stores, Kmarts, and Nordstroms. My nephew loves corn on the cob, and I came across the funkiest cob holders in a kitchenware catalog. Perfect. Memorable. And very unclelike.

Your presentation should be as unique as your gift. I have put tiny gifts into much bigger boxes, fooling my nieces and nephews about what they were going to receive. I have given cheap, disappointing plastic wallets filled with a surprise wad of dollar bills. I've used newspaper or torn up paper bags for wrapping paper. I've carried unwrapped small gifts in my pocket and just handed them over.

Where you give your gift counts, too. If it's personal, try somewhere quiet and alone, like on a walk or in a rowboat. If it's funky, do it at the dinner table with everyone around. Private? Make sure to close the door behind you.

Sometimes you can allow the gift itself to dictate the venue. Give a bowling ball, a new bat, or tap dancing shoes at the places they are used. Give a hooded fleece jacket outdoors on a cool night. Give a new backpack on the way to school.

Find excuses to give gifts. First tooth, first word, first step, or first day out with a car. Remember Valentine's day, Halloween, and Easter. And don't be afraid to surprise them with a gift on Groundhog day, President's day, or Albert Einstein's birthday. Sometimes, the excuse for the gift is as fun as the gift itself.

Get them subscriptions to magazines, newspapers, or journals; they educate and last all year. Consider enrolling them in a book of the month, fruit of the month, or nuts of the month club.

Determine their favorite company, cereal brand, or fast food and get anything with the logo on it.

What you spend on a gift is hardly a consideration, but creativity does count. Keep your mind open, allow inspiration to strike, and be spontaneous. When you see something that you know is right—buy it. Except for birthdays and special occasions, never arrive with a gift for just one of the kids, ignoring the others. Make sure you have something in hand for each. Don't buy a video unless you will watch it with them or a game unless you're willing to play. And if the kids buy you a gift, make believe you love it, even if you don't. "Just what I've always wanted," is a suitable response. And no matter what, wear it or use it the next time you see them.

THE ELEVEN GREATEST TOYS OF THE MILLENNIUM

1. The yo-yo
2. Legos
3. Crayola Crayons
4. Slinky
5. Play Doh
6. Etch-a-Sketch
7. Barbie
8. Frisbee
9. Matchbox cars
10. Teddy bears
11. Silly Putty

MILESTONES AND GIFT-GIVING

Here are some gift ideas to mark those special milestones—major and minor—throughout childhood:

Birth to One Year Old

Birth	A U.S. savings bond for college
Sleeps through the night	An alarm clock
Smiles	A mirror
Babbles	A tape recorder

Toddler

Learns to walk	A CD with marching music
Recognizes body parts	An anatomy chart
First drawing	A box of crayons
Dresses self with only minimal help	A sterling silver shoe horn

Preschool (3–6 years old)

Understands time	A pocket watch
Understands size	Matching big and small beach balls
Hops	A jump rope
Begins reading	Your favorite childhood book

School Age (6–12)

Loses first tooth	A leather pouch
Understands and follows directions	Karate lessons
Participates in a team sport	A uniform

Adolescent

Peer pressure	Clothes
Academic pressures	Concert tickets
Financial pressure	Cash
Opposite sex anxieties	A manicure set

MILESTONES AND GIFT-GIVING

Here are some gift ideas to mark those special milestones—major and minor—throughout childhood:

Birth to One Year Old

Birth	A U.S. savings bond for college
Sleeps through the night	An alarm clock
Smiles	A mirror
Babbles	A tape recorder

Toddler

Learns to walk	A CD with marching music
Recognizes body parts	An anatomy chart
First drawing	A box of crayons
Dresses self with only minimal help	A sterling silver shoe horn

Preschool (3–6 years old)

Understands time	A pocket watch
Understands size	Matching big and small beach balls
Hops	A jump rope
Begins reading	Your favorite childhood book

School Age (6–12)

Loses first tooth	A leather pouch
Understands and follows directions	Karate lessons
Participates in a team sport	A uniform

Adolescent

Peer pressure	Clothes
Academic pressures	Concert tickets
Financial pressure	Cash
Opposite sex anxieties	A manicure set

UNCLEDOTE

Grown Up At Last

AT LISA'S SWEET *sixteen birthday party, the family gathered round as Lisa opened her presents. She got a Discman from her brother Tony, a pair of outrageous sunglasses from their next-door neighbors, a book, a beautiful leather wallet, and a matching set of luggage from her parents. And last, in a box with no card, she found a sexy pair of white high-heeled shoes. Her first! Everyone oohed and aahed. Somebody whistled; Lisa blushed.*

It was from Uncle Peter, of course.

How To Tell a Story

YOU CAN'T GET around this one. Sooner or later, your nephews and nieces are going to ask for a story. If you don't oblige, they'll start to insist. If you don't agree, they'll begin to demand.

There are a couple of ways to deal with this. One is obvious: Pick up a book and read to them. Get them comfortably snuggled, point to pictures, be as dramatic as possible, and read out loud.

The problem is, I'm sure you will get bored. These books were written for kids, and whereas you might pick up on an author's cleverness or originality, it's unlikely you'll find them interesting.

Don't try skipping pages; they'll know. Don't try reading too fast; they'll whine. Don't forget to ask about the pictures; they'll realize. You've just got to sit through the book, beginning to end, and hope that they'll get bored first. Somehow, they never do.

But spinning a yarn or telling a story is an entirely different matter. Now you're on stage, testing your skills as a dramatist, projecting, improvizing, and commanding the attention of your audience.

And the stories can be true or made up, real or embellished. They can be yarns taken from current events or history. They can be mysteries, romances, cliff-hangers, or even to-be-continueds, where you tell them a new chapter from the same story each week.

My family has some favorite stories owned by uncles. There's one about the time my brother took a bad fall off a high chair on which he was playing judge, but didn't tell Mom he was hurt because she had said, "Don't come crying to me." We found bloody footsteps leading to the bathroom where he tried desperately to stop the bleeding from a wound on his chin that would eventually need eight stitches to close.

Or the time my sister and I ended up lost in Rockaway's Playland, miles from our home, the very day we moved to our new neighborhood.

Or what my brother did with one of my sister's tiny restraining rubber bands for her braces. I can tell you that he stopped the circulation to his private parts.

There are thousands of stories I could tell, about grandparents immigrating, relatives in foreign lands, trips through the desert, and first airplane rides. About bad grades, bad purchases, and bad deals. About mischief and virtues, and employers and cable repairmen. About arriving late, traffic accidents, and school plays. About first dates, blind dates, and commitment.

Everybody has a story to tell, and you won't find a better audience than your nephews and nieces. They're not likely to say, "I can top that one." They'll be too interested to interrupt. They're gullible, and they're appreciative.

What's the secret to telling a good story? It's all in the details.

Take a typical uncle story line about the time Mom brought home a D in history.

Where were Grandma and Grandpa when she showed it to them? In the kitchen? The living room? The garage? What were they doing? Reading the newspaper? Gardening? Paying bills? Which newspaper? What was the headline? What were they growing? What did a telephone call cost in those days? Did Mom beat around the bush, make up a story, or just put her report card on the table? What was her excuse? What kind of story did she make up? What did she say? What else was on the table?

What was everybody wearing? What time of day was it? Was it rainy or sunny? Dark or cloudy?

I think you get the idea. And this works for true stories as well as fabricated stories. Even if you're yarning a piece out of world history, the Cuban missile crisis or the exploits of Napoleon, you can add the word "probably." He probably wore red. It was probably bitter cold outside. It was probably fifty miles from Miami.

But be careful. You're going to be asked to tell the best of these stories again and again. Make sure the details match. You'll feel foolish when they say, "No, Unk. It was a red hat. A red hat."

Tell the story. Embellish the details. Put yourself in it and spin the yarn. Unlike reading books, you won't get bored. And each time you tell it, it's a whole new challenge.

Stay on your toes; perfect your delivery, and you'll be the most popular uncle around.

LIST OF UNCLE'S
FAVORITE READING

PICTURE BOOKS FOR PRESCHOOLERS:

1. *Three Billy Goats Gruff*
   P.C. Asbjornsen

2. *Goodnight Moon*
   Margaret Wise Brown

3. *The Very Hungry Caterpillar*
   Eric Carle

4. *Gingerbread Boy*
   Paul Galdone

5. *Anansi the Spider*
   Gerald McDermott

6. *The Tale of Peter Rabbit*
   Beatrix Potter

7. *The Snowy Day*
   Ezra Jack Keats

8. *Clifford the Big Red Dog*
   Norman Bridwell

9. *Hush Little Baby*
   Sylvia Long

10. *I am a Bunny*
   Richard Scarry, Ole Risom

List of Uncle's Favorite Reading

Ages 4-8

1. *Madeline*
Ludwig Bemelmans

2. *Story of Babar*
Jean de Brunhoff

3. *Corduroy*
Don Freeman

4. *Where the Wild Things Are*
Maurice Sendak

5. *The Complete Adventures of Curious George*
Margaret Ray

6. *The Velveteen Rabbit*
Margery Williams Bianco

7. *Green Eggs and Ham*
Dr. Seuss

8. *The Complete Tales of Winnie-the-Pooh*
A. A. Milne

9. *Mike Mulligan and His Steam Shovel*
Virginia Lee Burton

10. *Eloise*
Kay Thompson

LIST OF UNCLE'S FAVORITE READING

AGES 9-12:

1. *Charlotte's Web*
   E.B. White

2. *Little Women*
   Louisa May Alcott

3. *The Secret Garden*
   Frances Hodgson Burnett

4. *Ramona the Pest*
   Beverly Cleary

5. *James and the Giant Peach*
   Roald Dahl

6. *The Black Stallion*
   Walter Farley

7. *The Lion, the Witch and the Wardrobe*
   C. S. Lewis

8. *The Phantom Tollbooth*
   Norton Juster

9. *The Jungle Book*
   Rudyard Kipling

10. *A Wrinkle in Time*
   Madeline L'Engle

★

The Gift of Song

WE DON'T SING enough in America. I don't mean singers on stage, in nightclubs, and on TV variety shows. We surely see enough of that.

I mean the average, normal individual. The average uncle. After all, when was the last time you really belted out a song? Was it in the shower? A place where nobody sees you and nobody hears you (or so you think)?

That's exactly the point. Uncles need not be great singers to sing to their nieces and nephews. Everyone knows that being an uncle is a great equalizer. If you simply let down your guard, as uncles can do, you can sing out anytime at the top of your lungs.

After all, what is it that you need to make funny faces at them, flub jokes and somersaults, eat sloppily with chopsticks, and squeeze them to death? You guessed it; a lack of inhibition. You would never act this way with your new girlfriend, your boss, or a community leader. But you do with a nephew or niece, because they allow you the comfort you need.

Singing is one of the great things uncles have to offer. Soft songs that lull babies to sleep, fun songs that make the kids want to join in, silly songs that make them laugh, popular songs they need to know, songs they learn at school, songs they learn on the streets.

Do you have to sing in order to be an uncle? No. But singing together is bonding. And bonding is what uncling is all about.

You don't need to know the lyrics. Nor do you even need a melody. Just sing and substitute Unk or Uncle for the lyric; sometimes include your niece or nephew's name. Improvise the rest with sounds.

Here's my version of "This Land Is Your Land:"

Oh Uncle Jesse, Oh Uncle Jesse,
Oh Uncle Jesse, Oh Uncle Jesse
Oh Uncle Jesse, Oh Uncle Jesse,
Uncle and Dani uncledoo.

Here's "Jingle Bells:"

Uncle Bill, Uncle Bill, Uncle Billydoo.
Sallygirl, Sally girl, Sally Sally doo.
Uncle Bill, Uncle Bill, Uncle Billydoo.
Sally, Sally, Sally girl, uncle doodle do.

The beauty is that you can pick songs that match the moment. Sing happy songs for fun, pop songs to entertain, or mellow songs to soothe. You can pretend there's a headset mike wrapped around your face. You can reach for notes you know you can't hit. You can mimic your favorites, from Springsteen to Sinatra. You can uncle, simply by leaving your inhibitions behind.

THE HISTORY OF POPCORN

HERE ARE SOME facts to share with your niece or nephew as you're waiting for a movie to start:

1. Popcorn was grown in China, Sumatra, and India years before Columbus visited America.

2. The oldest known corn pollen was found 200 feet below Mexico City in an 80,000-year-old fossil.

3. The oldest known ear of popcorn was discovered in a bat cave west of central New Mexico in 1948. It is about 5,600 years old.

4. On the east coast of Peru, researchers found grains of popcorn 1,000 years old. They can still pop.

5. When Columbus arrived in the West Indies, the locals tried to sell popcorn to the crew.

6. The Iroquois popped popcorn in a clay vessel and used it to make soup.

7. Native Americans brought popcorn to meetings with the colonists as a sign of goodwill.

8. Kernels of popcorn contain a drop of water inside a circle of soft starch surrounded by a covering of hard starch. As the kernel heats up, the water expands, pressure builds against the hard surface, and it pops.

9. Native Americans used to believe that a spirit who got angry when annoyed by heat lived inside the kernels. As the heat increased, they got angrier and angrier, shaking until they finally burst out and escaped in a puff of steam.

And don't think of singing as just entertainment for the kids. Singing is bonding. You might start off softly with only a few simple tunes, but as the kid gets older, you will both increase your repertoire, showing wider musical breadth, always using the uncle lyric. My nephew Avi, at thirty-one, still sings with me today, often ending lines in a falsetto opera voice.

When I sing, I usually try to match the mood, but sometimes I try to create the mood. I have a trick that I use, and it works well for me. There are lots of tunes I know that speak about the city of Jerusalem, using a variety of new or ancient lyrics. Some are about her beauty, some, her tragedy, some, her joy, and some, her future. Naturally, some are upbeat and others are not; some are welcoming, while some are mysterious. My personal feelings toward the city make me croon or feel the joy. And with so many themes to choose from, I can hardly go wrong.

Jerusalem works for me. But you can choose song themes of your own, anything from love, romance, heartbreak, or achievement. Choose an artist or an era you know and like; a CD or a Broadway show. Your singing will be more real, less silly. It will help you give the music meaning. It will help create the bond.

☆

TWELVE LULLABYES

1. "Hush Little Baby"
2. "Brahms' Lullabye"
3. "Sylvia" (Schubert)
4. "Now the Day Is Over"
5. "Twinkle Twinkle"
6. "We Will Rock You"
7. "Dreaming" (Schumann)
8. "All the Pretty Horses"
9. "Golden Slumbers"
10. "Bedtime"
11. "Kumbaya"
12. "Rock-a-Bye-Baby"

☆

EIGHT WAYS TO UNCLE

☆ ☆

Uncles touch lives.

AT ANY GIVEN time or place, an uncle must be prepared to fulfill different family needs and play different family roles. In my experience, there are eight key things you need to keep in mind in order to uncle effectively in any situation.

1. Give Kids Space

ESCAPE FOR A child is very important, but it demands a certain level of safety and security. It also requires that they let something go and leave it behind—even if only temporarily.

Uncling is a kid's escape from their everyday life and the tyranny of Mom and Dad.

Children are limited in their free space. They can go to the backyard and play, close the door to their room, or walk to the corner and back home. They can turn on a video, even read a book, but rarely do they have the opportunity to escape in the company of an understanding adult.

Periodically they go on play dates, usually highly supervised affairs that expose them to new but familiar adult relationships. Teachers, students, and neighbors make up their entire list of associates. Grandma and Grandpa do play a special role, but often a great deal of respect and restraint is necessary.

Kids need to get away, to let their hair down without caution, to be free of the burdens of their everyday roles as responsible children. You can let them out. You can let kids play their different, easier, but still very fulfilling role of nephew or niece.

As an uncle, you are close; close enough for confidences, sleepovers, and trips to the mountains. Yet you are free of the day-to-day struggles that develop between parents and children. Often you'll hear a kid say something like, "but Uncle Jerry rides a motorcycle, and he's your brother." You allow freer thought, independent thinking. You justify lifestyles.

You can get away with things, you have authority without the burden of upbringing, you side with the kids as much as you do with the parents. You break the mold formed by every other adult in their life.

Yes, slobbering over food, arriving late and unannounced, roughhousing with the kids until they are overtired, and flicking bottlecaps across the table are all negative role model behaviors. But they work for uncles, because they accentuate how different you are from Mom and Dad—how much you can get away with without being thrown out of the family, how many norms you can violate, how many rules you can break, and how many instructions you can ignore; all without sacrificing their love.

You don't have to take kids on vacations or invite them over for sleepovers. You don't need closed-door sessions or long thoughtful walks. While these are all valid uncling tools, you can provide a kid with an escape by just sitting across from your nephew at the family table or going to your niece's piano recital.

Surprise your nephews and nieces and share a confidence. Ask them for their advice and respect their opinions. Let them grow, by giving them the space they need. Let them be themselves when you're around.

Pretty soon it will be you they turn to when they need to escape for a while.

★

2. Give Mom and Dad
Rescue and Respite

AS AN UNCLE, you have no obligation to make life better for
a parent. You should realize that just by asking you for help,
they are probably hitting the bottom of the list of child-care
providers. If you feel used or resentful, just say no. A resentful
uncle contradicts the notion of a good uncle because he becomes
overwhelmed each time he sees his nephews and nieces.

Do try, however, to turn these requests into opportunities. A
parent's respite could be your perfect opportunity to bond. And
parents hold the strings in your relationships with the kids. You
want to be helpful and don't want to be adversarial.

This is especially true in emergencies. When my baby brother
was born, my father rushed my mother to the hospital and my
uncle came over to care for us. It was Unk who got to break the
news that it was a boy, not a monkey, as my father had teased;
a fond memory. The rescuer, savior, or last-minute solution is a
fairly typical role for responsible uncles to play. And unlike
respite, it benefits the kids as well as the parents.

Either way, expect the kids to be thrilled that you stay with
them. They've had enough of grandmas, aunts, and the gum-
snapping teenager from down the block. They will hardly think

of themselves as alone when you are there. But be careful: They probably have all kinds of plans for sabotage, including extended bedtimes, more TV, and even some roughhousing. Do whatever you want, but unlike most uncling visits, you can't just leave. You've got to see it through to the end, screaming repercussions and all.

If you do take on the challenge of caring for your nephews or nieces, one thing to consider is where you want to take care of them—your place or theirs. Surely, Mom will want them at her house; but I'll bet that both you and the kids would appreciate a trip to your place.

Be equipped for a visit to your home; have the right foods, the right toys, the right environment. If you're single or have no kids of your own, this can be quite a challenge. Make your home safe and welcome. Consider taking only one kid. Maybe you should stay at their house after all.

Parents who ask uncles to take over realize the risk. Believe me, if they had another choice they'd probably take it. If you feel up to it, do it. And remember, besides bonding with the kids, as an uncle you fulfill an important role in society.

Yes, uncles are expected to be spontaneous, not rigid. But it's best to allow respites to happen on your schedule, not theirs. "How about letting me take the kids to the circus next Tuesday night." That's respite, uncle-style.

CHILDPROOFING YOUR HOME

YOU NEED NOT take all of these steps, but be aware of the dangers they present:

1. Secure loose cords.
2. Cover electrical outlets.
3. Keep drawers closed and locked.
4. Cover your garbage can.
5. Put safety latches on lower bathroom cabinets.
6. Lock away your medicines.
7. Lock bathroom doors.
8. Hide matches and sharp utensils.
9. Put away household cleaners.
10. Secure bookcases to walls.
11. Get rid of any sex magazines or other inappropriate material.

Tips on Baby-Sitting

THERE'S NOTHING BETTER for kids than having someone as familiar as an uncle baby-sit. Here are some suggestions on how to handle your baby-sitting experience:

1. Ask if you can bring a friend.
2. Bring along your own music.
3. Rent two videos: one for you and the kids; one for later that night.
4. Don't stick to strict bedtimes—after all, you're an uncle—but do get them to bed.
5. Prepare a story they've never heard for bedtime.
6. Leave the teasing and roughhousing for another visit.
7. Don't do homework *for* the kids. Do it *with* them.
8. Find out what the kids like to eat and make sure the refrigerator is stocked.
9. Determine what you want to eat and make sure to bring it along.
10. Keep doors locked even if you usually don't.

3. Encourage

TO ENCOURAGE OR motivate, you first must determine exactly what action you want. You can encourage a decision, a purchase, an environment, or a career. You can encourage a lifestyle, a hobby, an activity, or a thought. But know that what you choose to encourage can make all the difference.

You can't really tell someone what to do or what action you think they should take. You can only create the environment that will allow for a decision.

Say, for example, you think your niece could develop her fascination with cameras into a full-fledged hobby or even avocation. You could buy her a camera, go on a photo shoot together, give her a gift certificate to a photo shop, take her to a photographic exhibit, introduce her to your photographer friend, enter her photos in a local newspaper contest, or ask her to take a portrait of you.

Clearly, none of these will actually turn her into a photographer. Only her skill and determination can do that. But that's exactly what encouragement is. It suggests rather than persuades; it offers opportunity rather than coerces. Surely, you could just tell your niece to be a photographer. But that would be as effective as asking someone to buy a can of soup when they already have one.

It's always better to allow a kid, or anybody, to arrive at a conclusion on their own, rather than handing them the conclusion. Yes, one plus one is two. But a more effective teaching method is to hold up one finger and then another and say, "How many fingers do I have up now?"

Encouragement means letting a kid decide for himself. You can offer opportunity and information, suggest and present alternatives, but telling a kid what to do will not encourage him at all.

Being on a kid's side, or at least not actually supporting a parent's point of view, can encourage. Uncles don't give a hard time over bad report cards, late night dates, or spilt milk. Depending upon your relationship, you might even share the story of Mom's two D's in the fourth grade or Dad's ski accident in college. That kind of information, too, can encourage.

Allowing trial and error will also encourage. Kids are intimidated by most adults and are often afraid to try new things or test new ideas. Uncles provide a less fearful platform. You are often the first adult to watch a kid bat lefty, perform a pirouette, climb a tree, or drive a stick shift. Your approval is expected, yet genuine and appreciated. It is encouraging.

Your success can motivate. Anticipatory socialization, the ability to see yourself in a certain role because someone you know and trust is in that role, offers real encouragement. A niece can dream of becoming a fashion designer because you work in the fashion business. Many a lawyer, doctor, and aerospace engineer has become who they are because of a cherished uncle. Just being yourself can be an encouragement, perhaps the greatest encouragement of all.

But to encourage, you must share. You can't be quiet about yourself, your job, or your personality. You can't sit back and let bad habits develop or fears take over. You must give of yourself. You must encourage. You must uncle.

TEN THINGS TO ENCOURAGE:

1. An activity

2. A thought

3. A decision

4. A lifestyle

5. A virtue

6. A career

7. A hobby

8. A performance

9. A restriction

10. Entrepreneurship

UNCLEDOTE

The Gift that
Encouraged a Change

TASH, A FRIEND *of my sister's, emigrated from Romania to New York in her teens in the late 1950s. It was a chore getting her Americanized. Although she still hasn't lost her accent, today she is a well-adjusted, well-educated suburban mom. But it took her a while to give up a particular custom from her life in Romania. For years, she refused to shave her legs or her underarms.*

Friends, parents, even a courageous neighbor tried to convince her. But nothing worked. It was too ingrained and changing was perhaps too drastic a step from the familiar.

It was Uncle Willy, who had emigrated a decade before, who saved the day. On her birthday he got her a gift, a Remington electric shaver for women. We never saw any leg or underarm hair on Tash again.

What Madison Avenue Can Teach Uncles About . . .

ENCOURAGEMENT: A Lesson from Campbell's Soup

Campbell's Soup ran some wonderful advertising years ago. Yet soup sales were not affected. Puzzled, they researched their market. What they found was that although consumers were enticed, the message to go out and buy Campbell's soup fell on flat ears. Why? Because many consumers had already bought the soup, but the cans sat unopened on their shelves. They had already made their purchase; why buy more?

Campbell's changed their message from encouraging a purchase to encouraging usage. New commercials urged consumers to take a can of Campbell's off the shelf, open it, heat it up, and enjoy. Eventually, sales increased.

ALLOWING KIDS TO COME TO THEIR OWN CONCLUSIONS: A Lesson from Allegheny Airlines

Back in my ad agency days, I was given the problem of filling up seats on Allegheny Airlines, a small regional airline that was later bought out by U.S. Air. Their problem? Safety perception.

The company made runs with small aircraft to little, unlikely places like Allentown, Pennsylvania, and Rochester, New York. Puddle jumpers, we called them. One high-level executive at the agency used to joke that whenever he got onboard he would pull a dime out of his pocket to tighten the screws on the window beside him.

But lack of safety was only a perception, hardly a reality. The F.A.A.

was as strict with them as with anyone else. At the same time, it was unlikely that a safety campaign would be effective. You'd be handing the consumer a conclusion, and not allowing them to come to it on their own. And the last thing a consumer wants to be told is that planes are safe.

Here was my solution: If the planes, even small planes, go to so many obscure little places, they probably have a pretty large fleet. They probably have more planes than most airlines, take off and land more often, and go to more locations. So we created an ad campaign that positioned them as a big airline with a huge fleet of planes, because the consumer associates being big with being safe. We gave the consumer the information they needed to decide that Allegheny was safe, and it worked. Allegheny's reputation for safety was restored.

YOU CAN'T ENCOURAGE THINGS THAT KIDS REALLY DON'T WANT: A Lesson from Betty Crocker

Consider the classic case of Betty Crocker's introduction of cake mixes in the 1950s. A phenomenal idea! You just add water, pop it into the oven, and *voila*, you have a delicious cake. A breakthrough! Marvelous!

But it didn't sell. America just wasn't ready for the lightening of homemaker duties that was about to engulf the country. A cake that required no work was too easy, too unmotherlike, and that was unacceptable. So Betty Crocker made a change: They took the egg out of the mix. The instructions then asked that you open the package, crack and beat an egg into the mix, and pop the mixture into the oven.

The product sold, and eventually the egg was added to the mix once again, but the lesson was learned: You can't get someone to do something they really don't want to do.

★

4. Connecting Generations

YOU ARE PERFECTLY perched on the family tree. Not as high up as Grandma and Grandpa, yet on a branch alongside Mom and Dad, an understandable relationship, especially for a child.

Kids know what a brother is, and you are Mom or Dad's brother. In-laws make the understanding a bit more complicated, but any family tree can explain that. Uncles, in their prominent yet removed position from the nuclear family, demonstrate a special role; closeness without intrusion; family, but outside the home.

You can share fond memories of great-grandparents, the old neighborhood, life in the seventies, or school days before computers. You can describe old family recipes, ancient TV shows, hula hoops, and Cabbage Patch Kids. Best of all, you can tell all of the childhood stories of your siblings, the history of your nephews' and nieces' parents.

Although Mom and Dad have surely told tales, even about you, you can fill in the gaps. What did their parents leave out? How true were the things they put in? You give the unedited, fuller, most-accurate version of family life; leaving out, of course, the things that make you look bad.

Grandparents sometimes play this role, but their point of view is different. "Wise" is the word I can think of when grandparents offer up the past to their grandchildren. It's been adulterated through the passage of time, touched by the eyes of age. The way an uncle shares history is different. You present it like it happened yesterday.

Play an active role in keeping the family together. Consider maintaining a family Web site. When a new baby arrives, scan pictures and post them quickly. List milestones, anecdotes, facts, and trips. Encourage e-mailing and document sharing. Post artwork and finger painting. Upload videos and original music. Create links to interesting sites.

Buy a genealogy program and create a family tree with the kids. Look up Ellis Island documents, such as ship arrival dates and naturalization papers. Get out a map and show them the Old Country. Point out cities, changed boundaries, and locations of global conflicts and local feuds.

Take the kids through history and show them where your family originates. How far back can you go? The American Revolution? The Civil War? World War II?

Which presidents did Grandma and Grandpa vote for? What events did they live through? What effects did these things have on their lives?

Separate family fact from legend. Did Grandma really work as a barmaid? Was Mom expelled from high school? Was Dad a whiz on the pool table?

CREATE AN UNCLE WEBSITE

1. Give your Web site a name with the word "uncle" in it.

2. Make your site password protected so that only your nephews and nieces may gain access.

3. Send out e-mail invitations to your nephews and nieces to visit the site. Write the e-mail in your own special style.

4. Have a changing family photograph, or a changing photograph of yourself on the home page of your site.

5. Acknowledge birthdays and milestones.

6. Have a news box about the cousins.

7. Build a family tree and invite everyone to add their individual ancestry.

8. Set up a chat line for nieces and nephews (and you, of course).

9. Offer links to interesting sites you find.

10. Post an uncle's advice column for nephews and nieces only.

11. Offer a weekly uncle challenge.

12. Keep your Web site fresh. Update it regularly.

If you would like to have a free, password-protected site created just for you, go to www.myfamily.com and follow the instructions.

Drive the kids past old addresses, and visit old neighbors. Buy the foods you used to eat, the books you used to read. Collect old documents, such as report cards, drivers' licenses, and college acceptance letters.

Revitalize a family album. Retouch pictures to get rid of old cracks. Blow them up or add color to black-and-white photos.

Make yourself the one-stop source for family history. Nobody can pass it on in a less biased, more interesting, or more compelling manner than you.

5. Make Kids Proud

PRIDE SHOULD BE a feeling derived from someone else's achievement, a completely selfless feeling. It forms a connection with someone else and creates a bond with success.

Have you ever heard a kid say, "My uncle's a cop, and he'll come arrest you," or "My uncle's an astrophysicist, and he's smarter than anybody"? That's pride. That's a kid making his uncle his own.

Uncles are cool. Kids are proud of the clothes you wear, the car you drive, the way you pay for a Carvel ice cream. They think your career is great and your restaurant choices and girlfriends out of this world. But they also often feel incapable of making you equally proud. That is why some kids develop a sense of hero worship of their uncles.

Are kids proud of their parents? Sure, but more selectively. They hold back pride because they believe it has expectations attached. If Dad can belt a ball out of the ballpark, maybe I should be able to also. If he's a great orator, I shouldn't have stage fright. And if their achievements make them different from their parents, even in a positive way, kids might choose to squirm instead of beam.

I went to a Jewish elementary school where most of the parents were Holocaust survivors, anxious to start their lives over in a new land. My parents were in New York during the war; my father was born in Brooklyn. They were educated beyond college, articulate, and successful: worthy of my pride. But when my friends came over to my house (we didn't have play dates back then), they would wonder at our American lifestyle. I squirmed because I felt different. Even when my mother became president of the PTA, I was uncomfortable. It took years before the discomfort turned into pride.

If my father talked too loud, wolfed down his food, or forgot to change his socks, he easily slipped a notch in my esteem. The fact that I was to become a clone of him, as the years marched on, didn't make a difference to me. Anything out of the norm made me cringe. And how proud can you be of someone who makes you cringe?

Uncles, even with their quirks and unacceptable behaviors, make kids proud. They can wear cheap suits, make obscene jokes, and blow cigar smoke in their faces, and kids will still be proud of them. For Dad, on the other hand, kids want the best clothes, a perfect sense of humor, and clean-smelling breath. Perhaps it's because uncles are less of a reflection on them than their parents are. Perhaps it's the ambivalent feeling every child has toward his family. Perhaps it's because an uncle asks nothing in return.

Being the source of pride is equally invigorating. By your actions, you bring joy; a great fringe benefit of being an uncle.

At my nephew Avi's wedding, he approached me with two other men in their twenties. "This is my uncle Jesse," he said.

"*The* uncle Jesse?" they asked.

"*The* uncle Jesse," he said.

UNCLEDOTE

Surprise Finish

ALAN RAN THE *New York Marathon, not in recent years with all the hullabaloo, but in the formative 1970s when the path was open and not roped off as it is today, when the finish line was unbarricaded.*

He was not a professional runner by any means, but he did train, and he talked about it with his nephews. On the day of the marathon he felt good and ready to go. He felt gratified on the run through the boroughs as he watched his months of training pay off. His concentration was fierce; his determination intact. But a surprise startled him about a mile before the finish line.

"Alan. Uncle Alan."

Two proud nephews waited on the side line, dressed in running shoes and shorts, excited over their uncle's achievement. Soon Alan was flanked on either side, and together they crossed the finish line.

★

6. Love

LOVE IS ALLOWING a person to be himself, accepting imperfections, not trying to change them. Love makes no demands. Can you think of a better way to uncle?

7. Model Virtues and Values

WHETHER YOU PUSH homework or truancy, sports or gambling, books or bikinis, whether you introduce your nephews to good cigars, single malts, or bad dinner habits, you model virtues. Virtues, those universal ideas that society accepts, too often distorted by parents with their constant comparisons and demands, are gold in the hands of uncles.

I am not encouraging irresponsible behavior; certainly nothing immoral or forbidden. Sporting a tiny bikini, gambling, feeding video machines, and instilling a "speak when you're spoken to" mentality are certainly not activities appreciated by everyone. Ultimately it's the parents, not the uncle, who are responsible for instilling virtues and values.

But it's important to know that virtues go beyond mere behavior. Yes, truancy is inherently wrong, even if it is designed to see an afternoon movie with your niece or nephew. But truancy can encourage independence, and independence is a virtue.

Single-malt scotch consumed at the right age and in moderation is not necessarily bad. It's so superior to cheaper blends that older nieces and nephews may learn to appreciate another virtue: Excellence.

You can scale a mountain and encourage achievement.

Playing "who has the most watermelon seeds" at the table encourages competition.

"Let's be bad today," I would announce to my two nephews as we secretly planned to smother Mom's carefully prepared cuisine with mustard and ketchup. And they learned loyalty and comraderie.

"You're doing a terrible job of caring for that mutt," admonishes an uncle, modeling caring and responsibility.

"I bet I can climb that mountain better than you ever could." Courage. Achievement.

As long as you don't disrupt strongly held ideas, you can model whatever you want.

But don't choose virtues or values you don't personally hold dear. Why encourage loyalty if you can't keep a confidence, cleanliness if you're a slob? Let your modeling of values come naturally. Don't try to control them.

As long as you don't violate the value systems of your siblings, go for it. Take the kids to the beach, a mosque, or a video arcade. Stuff them with popcorn, potato chips, or astrology. Be free. Be yourself. Share the values for which you really stand.

MODEL, NEVER PREACH

DAN, A FORTUNE 500 executive, frequents the best restaurants in town, indulges in expensive cigars, and has his clothes custom made. But he did what caring uncles do, at one time or another. He took his nephews to McDonalds.

With two Big Macs and a milkshake under their belts and a portion of onion rings gone, it was time to head back home. The kids skipped to the door—just like in the commercials, loving every minute spent with their Uncle Dan—but left a ketchupy mess with their used cups and plates strewn all over the table. They ignored the people at the exit who dutifully lined up at the tray dropoff and refuse receptacle.

Dan returned to the table and wiped it up, taking his time to leave it spotless. He deposited the waste.

UNCLE LEO ESCORTED his sister Joyce and his nephew Sammy to the local sandbox. Sammy came well equipped with three different size shovels, a red sifter, two pails, and a set of animal molds. Leo, always ready to be a kid again, decided to join his nephew and get down and dirty. They filled and refilled pails, imagined a mountain instead of a molehill, destroyed it, and started over again. Joyce watched and chuckled.

But when a cute four-year-old approached and politely asked whether he could use Sammy's elephant mold, Sammy brushed him aside. Leo took two of the animal molds and a shovel over to the rejected boy and neatly filled a mold. Sammy soon followed, missing his uncle's attention.

UNCLEDOTE

Financial Independence

ON A COOL SUMMER day, I took my nephew Dani, then six years old, to one of America's largest outdoor flea markets. Located on the asphalt of Aqueduct Racetrack's parking lot, it featured a lot more than green depression glass. Among hundreds of other items, there was underwear, hardware, toy trucks, and plant stands, all lined up for as far as you could see. Turn a corner and there was the perfect fishbowl; turn again and there was a well-oiled baseball glove.

Dani marveled. He was well trained to avoid the "Can I have this or can I have that" routine. But his eyes popped at the array; his temptations were tested.

I pulled out a twenty-dollar bill and gave it to him. I explained that he could buy something that costs twenty dollars, two things that cost ten dollars each, four things that cost five dollars, or any combination thereof. I also told him that he could choose to pocket any or all of the money.

Puzzled, he started moving around the aisles, stopping to look, determined to spend his money in the best possible way.

"How much is this?" he would want to know.

"Ask the man," I would tell him.

"Could I get three of these?"

"Sure, but you'll have to give back one of the other things you bought," I explained.

To watch Dani decide where to go, making his own decisions, giving up one thing for another, considering cost versus need, was exciting. It was drama. It was damn good uncling.

UNCLEDOTE

Piety

THERE IS A *famous custom at Jewish weddings to break a glass at the end of the ceremony. The reason? To remind Jews of the sadder times amidst their joy, such as the destruction of the temple in Jerusalem, the suffering through the generations, and even family tragedies that remain in our memories. Jews spend a lot of time remembering.*

Some people need more ritual than others, however. In addition to the basic breaking of the glass, some Jews do something you've probably never seen. They put ash on the foreheads of the bride and groom. This has the same symbolism as breaking the glass, though is perhaps a bit more personal. Nevertheless, it's reserved for the small percentage of Jews, usually only the very fervent, who deem it proper. There are few Jewish weddings that leave out the glass. Most leave out the ash.

At his niece's wedding, Uncle Yosh was given an honor and approached the wedding canopy with dignity, placing himself right next to the young couple. As the glass was to be broken, in that beautiful moment when reflection turns to joy, when memories of the past turn to thoughts of the present, Yosh stepped forward and slapped some ash on the couple's foreheads.

> *Nobody knew where Yosh got the ash. Everyone was just angry and embarrassed. Yosh was a little too pious, everyone agreed, even if he was a favored uncle.*

MODELING VIRTUES

◆ **ASSERTIVENESS**	Say "no" sometimes, especially when they beg for a gift.
◆ **CHARITY**	Make a day out of delivering your old clothes to the Salvation Army.
◆ **GRATITUDE**	Send thank-you cards when they do something nice.
◆ **FORGIVENESS**	Say the words, "I was wrong."
◆ **DETERMINATION**	Teach your niece how to ice-skate.
◆ **FRIENDSHIP**	Spend some time alone with each of your nephews and nieces.
◆ **TRUTHFULNESS**	Show your nephew your high school report card.
◆ **COURAGE**	Coach your nephew in standing up to a bully.

THE TIME OUT:
NO WAY FOR AN UNCLE TO ACT

TIME OUT, A current disciplinary action, takes a child away from the action and puts him or her in a quiet place, alone, to cool down.

There are variations that range from allowing toys to be played with and TV to be watched to complete silence. When the child is ready, or after a specified amount of time, he or she is allowed to return.

This may be a good discipline technique for parents, when it works, but it's no way for an uncle to act. Leave the disciplining to the parents and put up with a little acting out for a while. Return the kids to their parents as soon as you lose control.

8. Validation:
The Greatest Gift You Can Give

UNCLES HAVE ALWAYS been boosters of children's esteem. You can see it in the confidence kids show when their uncles are around; in their delight, their passion, their zeal, their enthusiasm, their willingness to try new things, and their attempts to reach new goals.

And why not? Uncles have no expectations; their love is unconditional. They read with animation, watch TV with no regard to bedtime, and look at report cards without dire thoughts about college admission. At the same time, they are quasiparents; they don't have complete authority, just some authority. In the words of my friend Charlie, a professor of sociology, they are "other, but the same"; a fatherly figure that represents a looser version of authority.

From practical jokes to an evening of black jack, uncles are hardly models of correct behavior. Yet in the role of validator they excel. There is no statistic, but if there were, uncles would probably score the best, better than moms, dads, sisters, brothers, or teachers, on a booster of self-esteem evaluation. How could they miss? They aren't around consistently enough to demand anything. Yet they are as loyal and loving as anyone on earth.

HOLLYWOOD'S UNCLE

ONE OF THE warmest uncle relationships I know was depicted in the recent film release *You Can Count on Me*. Uncle Billy goes to the home of his divorced sister, takes his little nephew to a bar, shoots pool with him late into the night, and introduces him to the father he had never met. Everything Uncle Billy did was wrong, motivated by a complicated relationship with his sister. But he encouraged trust, and that made him an uncle worth cherishing.

While experts say self-esteem is the single most important factor in determining the success of a child, parents seem to always mess it up. And they know it. Just look at any current magazine article or book about parenting. Whole volumes are dedicated to the subject, and the Web is filled with information. Instilling self-esteem in kids has become an entire industry, complete with its own language, codes, and euphemisms. There are books, lectures, and music designed to increase self-esteem. There are seminars, how-to demonstrations, posters, toys, and clothing.

Why?

Because most parents compare, demand excellence, hold back praise, and say all the wrong things. Because parents don't understand that they can't coerce behavior. They mix up love with control, their need for excellence rather than their kid's preferences. Everything that emerges from a parent's mouth today—from schoolwork to sports and bedtime to barbecues—is either absolutely guarded and correct or a targeted sting that pierces the esteem and wounds the child.

"You are a bad boy," says the young mother, blind to its effect on the future success of her little boy.

"You are a good boy who does some bad things," says another mom, guardedly.

Some of this misbehavior has to do with expectations that are unreasonable; often it has to do with a misguided sense of motivation. My father grudgingly applauded a ninety-nine on my report card; he wanted to know why I didn't get a perfect one hundred. My mother insisted I eat more and more as a kid; later she lectured me on taking inches off my waistline.

These stories are anything but uncommon. But in all fairness, most of us were born in the days when self-esteem was hardly a consideration; my mom still thinks it's a disguise for being selfish.

I am not of the school of thought that dictates uncles need to watch every syllable they utter the way parents do. An uncle's bond, so lacking in negatives, so filled with trust and loyalty, lets you skip through the psychology of decoding and say what you want. Parents are too involved with parenting to be real with their kids. Uncles can be who they are.

Take an objective look at the dynamics of your sibling's family, and choose some areas you can affect. Does the family dress nicely, act honestly, show respect? In your role as confidant or skill provider, you can make a difference.

Although uncles are usually not the first to spot a baby's first tooth, they are often the first to notice the effects of the passage of time; that someone has grown, slimmed down, or matured; that someone reads faster, hits harder, or has grown more attractive.

Buy your niece her first *Cosmopolitan* or a hip-hugging outfit. Buy your nephew a bottle of aftershave. Get them lip gloss, a jock strap, or bath oils. Take them to a meeting, carbon copy them on a business e-mail, or take them out for a night on the town. Validate them, approve of them. Be the family member who really understands. That's what boosting self-esteem is really about.

Guide, don't judge; listen, don't preach. There are moments when kids simply need some objective love, unhindered by external and internal demands. You can provide it.

UNCLEDOTE

I Want To Dance Again

MOM WANTED JILL *to take ballet lessons. She tried all the psychology she knew. She pointed to the advantages of discipline, dexterity, talent, creative pursuit, and just trying something new. Nothing worked.*

Jill mistrusted her Mom; it seemed more like something Mom wanted than something she wanted. She refused to practice, read ballet books, or put ballet posters on her wall. Sometimes she would blurt out that she was simply not good at it. That was when Mom insisted that was because she never worked hard enough at anything.

Along came Uncle Jay with two tickets to the American Ballet. "Let me show you how it's really done," he said. Eagerly the ballet rejecter marked the date on her calendar. Uncle and niece had a grand time, topped off with ice cream sundaes on the way home.

The next morning over oatmeal Jill said, "You know, Mom, those dancers were great. Do you think I could ever be that good?"

A Lesson from
a Salesman

REMEMBER UNCLE BEN in "Death of a Salesman"? Willie Loman was particularly affected by his wealthy brother, who showed up every couple of years for no more than two hours at a time, always sharing the same message. "When I was sixteen," he would say, "I went into the jungle and came out a rich man." Uncle Ben showed no consideration for Willie, who felt he was a failure as a provider.

Be cautious. Never make a parent look foolish.

Uncles should consider the self-esteem of parents as well as children. Unlike parents, uncles ultimately have no responsibility for outcomes. They can complement or substitute, but not replace. And besides, hurt feelings and sibling rivalries could cause you to lose your access to the kids.

UNCLEDOTE

The Drummer

SIXTEEN-YEAR-OLD *Jeremy became a drummer in a rock band. They called him Jerms. To his parents' dismay, he dressed and looked the part. He was also out too late on weekends, practiced too loudly in a neighbor's garage, and bounced around the house tapping out new rhythms on the family dining-room table. With a Walkman in his ears, taking care of his needs, he would drum on the bathroom sink counter.*

First, Jeremy's parents declared it a passing and even interesting phase. But soon Mom and Dad got more and more anxious. Jeremy's grades dropped. And although she always promised herself that she would encourage the creative pursuits of her children, Jeremy's mom couldn't help but discourage the drumming.

"A drummer!" she exclaimed in horror. "A drummer?"

Jeremy's Uncle Richard, never Dick or Richie, was not exactly the creative type. A rising star at an important investment bank, he showed up regularly for Sunday afternoon lunch at Jeremy's house in striped suit and suspenders. And it wasn't just the way he dressed. It was his entire personality.

Richard listened to his sister's tale of woe about Jeremy's drumming. Somehow, even with his conservative perspective, he couldn't share her concern. Although he despised rock and roll, he had an uncle's faith in his nephew. As far as Richard was concerned, Jeremy could do no wrong. A drummer? So what? Jeremy will figure it out. He's probably enjoying every minute of it. Outwardly, of course, Richard shared his sister's anxieties.

The next Friday night, Richard explained to his girlfriend that he would have to start the night's activities a bit later than planned. Unaccompanied, he steered his BMW to a loud club located next to the tracks of a suburban commuter railroad station. He had spotted a flyer on Jeremy's cluttered wall announcing the band's appearance there.

Although Richard thought he would cause a stir walking into this loud, smoke-filled hall packed with teenagers, he didn't. The attention and screams of the masses were devoted exclusively to the stage where Jeremy intensely beat out the rhythm along with four of his friends. "Jerms! Jerms!" they screamed when Jeremy had his solo.

With a Coke in hand, Richard took a seat off to the side, away from the crowd. He watched Jeremy pound away for more than twenty minutes before he caught his eye. When Jeremy saw him—for a brief moment—a big smile broke out on his face. Richard raised his glass in a toast. Minutes later, he quietly slipped away to meet his girlfriend.

SPECIAL WAYS TO SHOW YOUR IN-LAW NEPHEWS AND NIECES YOU LOVE THEM:

- Include them in photographs.
- Always say "our" nephews and nieces, never "yours" or "mine."
- Take them out alone, without your wife.
- Take them out together with your blood nephews and nieces.
- Get into family photographs with them alone, without your wife.

7

THE UNCLE
RITE OF PASSAGE

*Marriage has its rings, its veils, its commitments. Graduation
has its silly hats and gowns. Religion has its Bar Mitzvahs and
baptisms. New Year's Eve has its hats and noisemakers. Mothers
and fathers have their day.*

But what about uncles?

RITES OF PASSAGE mark important changes in one's life.
And uncles deserve one of their own.

I could dream up any number of rituals that might fit the bill.
You could prick a balloon with a sterling silver pin engraved
with the baby's name or publicly pinch the newborn, twice on
each cheek, followed with a quick grabbing of the nose and a loving kiss to the forehead. Maybe uncles should perform a
rehearsed magic trick designed to show commitment, responsi-

bility, and skill. Or release a loud public belch to an audience of family and friends.

Practically speaking, however, it should be less complicated and require no particular skill, designed simply to memorialize an uncle's undertaking. It should provide motivation for the uncle himself and publicly announce his commitment. A respectful observance. A celebration.

Who should come? How lavish? What should be served? These concerns are as relevant to an uncle party as they are to planning a wedding; cocktails, snacks, or a sit-down dinner; live band or just conversation; two hundred guests or ten. But it's the objective of the party, not its execution, that really matters. You still graduate from high school whether your diploma is a rolled and ribboned piece of parchment or a handsomely mounted flat piece of paper.

There should be some uniform identifying factor to the celebration. And with all the celebratory activity surrounding a baby's arrival, the congratulations all focused on parents and grandparents and long established parenting rites of passage so firmly rooted in society, an uncle party would hardly seem a welcome addition. But the right timing can make all the difference.

Baby's First Birthday: The Uncle Party

WHY HAVE AN uncle's party on baby's first birthday?

1. The venue of a first birthday party is unimportant. A baby is hardly aware of this milestone, and unlike a six- or seven-year-old's party, where the place and the guests make all the difference, a first birthday party by an uncle would hardly have an affect on the child's emotional development. First birthdays are more of a celebration for adults, anyway.

2. Most uncles have done little uncling by this point, and limited bonding has taken place. Their relationship is about to be become more interactive as this milestone is met, and it's an appropriate time for an uncle to demonstrate his commitment.

3. First birthday parties are already accepted celebrations within society, already an established moment to mark. It would be easy to allow uncles to own the moment, since the celebratory concept doesn't change, just the host and the family member responsible for the festivities.

4. Since there is often more than one interested uncle, commitments could be shared, giving new opportunity for extended family bonding.

5. It's a great excuse for a party.

★

Beyond Rites of Passage

IN THE HEIGHT of the 1960s, as part of a youth culture that denounced materialism, commercialization, and institutionalization, I bucked the system and refused to send my Mom a Mother's day card. "Ridiculous commercialism," I insisted. "Created by the department stores to sell gifts; by Hallmark to sell cards; by the garment center to boost the economy." My mother cried.

Once, because the spirit moved me, I sent a Father's day card to my mother's father on Father's day that expressed, from the heart, how much I loved him. When he died, that card was found in a wooden box where he kept his cherished things.

Secretaries demanded their day and got it. So did valentines. Yet uncles, perhaps most cherished of all, have no day to call their own.

Sure it's commercialism. And like the sale of flowers and chocolates, so might it skyrocket the sale of sporting goods and men's accessories. But see beyond the commercialism to my mother's tears and my grandfather's treasures. There is a need to acknowledge and be recognized, adore and be cherished, especially when your relationship is all too often taken for granted.

Uncle's day, like Father's day, could be a day out with the family. Like breakfast in bed on Mother's day and a tie on Father's day, traditions would develop for celebration. Uncles, good or bad, devoted or absent, would finally get their due.

Ideas for
Homemade Uncle Day Cards

For the Long-Distance Uncle

You live so far away,

We hardly get to play.

But whether you're here

Or way over there,

You're my uncle.

I'd have it no other way.

For the Dedicated Uncle

Some uncles are taken for granted.

Some hardly come through.

But you're always there,

A big huggy bear.

I love you, I love you, I do.

☆

Suggestions on How To Spend Uncle Day

- Alone with the kids, without their parents.

- At a brunch in your apartment or at a restaurant of your choice.

- Doing something you'll all enjoy; not an activity specifically designed to entertain the kids.

- Making plans with a few other uncles and taking all the kids out together.

☆

AFTERWORD

DEBBIE, A COMPULSIVE *packrat and reader of magazines, books, and specialized articles, visited with her eighty-one-year-old Uncle Zelig one last time in his book-lined home library. Imposing titles were scattered throughout; journals and clippings were piled high. Debbie had long realized that her uncle was the source of her sponge-like need for information and insight. Perhaps nobody had shaped her intellectual life more.*

Her request was personal and emotional. She asked Uncle Zelig for something of his. Something she could cherish long after he was gone, like a book, an article, or a rare magazine.

Zelig handed Debbie a handwritten journal he had secretly kept over the years. It was filled with fragmented lines and scribbles.

"All these years, I never knew you wrote poetry, Uncle Zelig," Debbie said in awe, as she lovingly touched the pages of her prize.

"And all these years, I never knew how much an effect I had on your life," replied Uncle Zelig. There were tears in his eyes.

My nephew Avi called me from Israel. He was eighteen years old and had been agonizing over what his college major should be. He called to say he had finally decided, and that I was the first to know.

"Unk, I'm going to major in communications, like you," he announced. Eventually, he became a respectable journalist.

Dani called me, equally excited, a couple of years later. He was determined to be a photographer. "Maybe I'll be able to do some work for your ad agency," he said with a smile. Today he is the staff photographer for Ben Gurion University in the Negev.

The family said that I was Avi and Dani's greatest influence. I'm not really sure of that. I know, and Avi and Dani know, that neither journalist nor photographer is the same as an advertising creative director.

But I did come to realize the effect I had on their lives.

Our family had high but narrow expectations of its members: We were expected to become doctors, lawyers, or businessmen; or maybe a computer programmer or perhaps a college professor. But earning a living from an enjoyable talent was hardly encouraged; it was almost frowned upon.

I changed that when I went to work on Madison Avenue. My career was solid, I had the respect of the community, and my earnings were respectable. I gave my nephews the freedom to choose; if their uncle could do it, why couldn't they?

I had offered them the space away from their family they needed in order to make that choice. I encouraged them to explore their talents and gave them the confidence to try them out. They were proud of me; I knew that all along. But realizing how their pride translated into action made me swell with pride and happiness.

Uncles have lots to offer, but they also get a lot in return. The bond is unique, and it can last a lifetime. Live up to your role; it will make your days sweeter and richer.

I married four years ago, for the first time, at the age of forty-six. Naomi, besides being my best friend, has also brought me a wonderful new set of nephews and nieces.

A month ago, we adopted twins. I now hold, burp, change diapers, and feed. I've bonded with Max and Riva already, and I must admit it's very different from being an uncle.

But the biggest joy in our new family came from my siblings and my nephews and nieces. My older brother, Hirsh, and his wife, Irene, were among our biggest helpers. Through our kids, they have shown a love and commitment never exhibited before. Perhaps, like my sister and I, they needed a next generation to bond with.

My sister flew in from Israel, all teary eyed. She wouldn't miss the excitement for the world. We felt closer than ever.

Will I still be as close with my nephews and nieces? You bet! Because I have something to give that I never had to give them before. Cousins. One more extension of the family. One more reason to uncle.

ACKNOWLEDGMENTS

ALTHOUGH MY EXPERIENCES as an uncle are rich and many, I couldn't have written *The Uncle Book* without the stories and input of the many uncles whom I interviewed both officially and informally throughout the last two years. I thank all of them.

One of the uncles, Alan Leicht, was especially helpful in making this book happen. He shared its vision, along with his wife, Renee, from its inception, read the manuscript, recognized the bunkle as the name for an uncle's special bond and shared some very loving and anguishing moments of being an uncle. Alan, along with Renee, did what uncles do best—they encouraged me.

Charlie Selengut, a professor of sociology, with whom I've spent hours and hours solving the problems of the world in the back row of my parents' synagogue, was crucial in forming, guiding, and shaping insights into the uncle's role in society. As always, his book intelligence coupled with unusual street smarts served as an important stimulus in writing this book.

Another professor of sociology, Sid Langer, surprised his criminology students one day by handing out pieces of paper and asking them to jot down thoughts about their uncles off the top of their heads. The results were telling and amusing, and helped confirm many of my premises for this book.

A number of my friends in publishing were forced to live through years of my boasting that I would write this book and my constant and probably annoying updates. Especially good sounding boards were Sandee Brawarsky and Sarah Brzowsky. Thank you for listening, criticizing, and encouraging.

Two people who "got" this book from the beginning were Robert Shepard, my literary agent, and Matthew Lore, my editor at Marlowe. Robert became a good long-distance friend, sharing much more than just publishing. Matthew read my first draft, ripped it apart, gave me new direction and turned it into a better, more reader-friendly book. Both Robert and Matthew made themselves available as loving uncles in addition to their roles as editor and agent. Thank you both.

Sue McCloskey, who read and corrected my manuscript word by word and line by line, was great. Thanks! You "got" it, too.

I also thank everyone involved in the design and production of this book, including Jahoo Glinski for his striking care, Pauline Neuwirth for her interior page design, and Ghadah Alrawi

A few people read the early drafts of my manuscript and I'd like to thank all three. My wife, Naomi, my mother, and my mother-in-law (yes, my mother-in-law!). Their expertise and insights into family relationships were important to me. A special thanks to Mom and Naomi for censoring some of the personal family material. You were right.

Elyakeem Erin Kinstlinger, who is a partner in everything I do, was right there for me during this project. Either by taking on some of the tasks I couldn't manage while writing, or by researching and making suggestions, Erin, as usual, came through one hundred percent.

One of my uncles, Uncle Mark, died during the process of publishing of this book. He was a man of stature in the circles I traveled and many knew me simply as his nephew and I was proud of that. Although his reputation as a principal in a major private Jewish institution was strict and unforgiving, he was a caring, joking, and available uncle. My relationship with him offered much material for this book. I will miss him.

Uncle Jack, or Unk, still very much alive, was a constant inspiration for *The Uncle Book*. His personal guidance, openness, honesty, and love have made and continue to make a difference in my life. If there was a model for the perfect uncle, it was he. I cherish every moment we have spent together.

And of course, my nephews and nieces, both blood and in-law. Avi and Elisheva, Dani, Yonina, and Elad; Jen, Jon, and Jason; David and Bonnie, Danny, Nava, Rachel, and Avi. Also my grandnephews and nieces: Penina, Yoni, Ayelet Nitzan, Ahava Yakir, and Ori. I tested my uncling on all of them. Each taught me something and each played a part in the writing of this book. I love you all.

CPSIA information can be obtained at www.ICGtesting.com
Printed in the USA
LVOW092133300512

283879LV00001B/13/A